Undoing Networks

IN SEARCH OF MEDIA

Timon Beyes, Mercedes Bunz, and
Wendy Hui Kyong Chun, Series Editors

Action at a Distance
Archives
Communication
Machine
Markets
Organize
Pattern Discrimination
Remain
Undoing Networks

Undoing Networks

Tero Karppi, Urs Stäheli, Clara Wieghorst,

and Lea P. Zierott

IN SEARCH OF MEDIA

University of Minnesota Press
Minneapolis
London

meson press

In Search of Media is a collaboration between the University of Minnesota Press and meson press, an open access publisher, https://meson.press.

Published by the University of Minnesota Press, 2021
111 Third Avenue South, Suite 290
Minneapolis, MN 55401-2520
https://www.upress.umn.edu

in collaboration with
meson press
Salzstrasse 1
21335 Lüneburg, Germany
https://meson.press

ISBN 978-1-5179-0669-6 (pb)
A Cataloging-in-Publication record for this book is available from the Library of Congress.

UMP BmB 2021

Contents

Series Foreword

"Media determine our situation," Friedrich Kittler infamously wrote in his Introduction to *Gramophone, Film, Typewriter*. Although this dictum is certainly extreme—and media archaeology has been critiqued for being overly dramatic and focused on technological developments—it propels us to keep thinking about media as setting the terms for which we live, socialize, communicate, organize, do scholarship, et cetera. After all, as Kittler continued in his opening statement almost thirty years ago, our situation, "in spite or because" of media, "deserves a description." What, then, are the terms—the limits, the conditions, the periods, the relations, the phrases—of media? And, what is the relationship between these terms and determination? This book series, *In Search of Media,* answers these questions by investigating the often elliptical "terms of media" under which users operate. That is, rather than produce a series of explanatory keyword-based texts to describe media practices, the goal is to understand the conditions (the "terms") under which media is produced, as well as the ways in which media impacts and changes these terms.

Clearly, the rise of search engines has fostered the proliferation and predominance of keywords and terms. At the same time, it has changed the very nature of keywords, since now any word and pattern can become "key." Even further, it has transformed the very process of learning, since search presumes that, (a) with the right phrase, any question can be answered and (b) that the answers lie within the database. The truth, in other words, is "in there." The impact of search/media on knowledge, however, goes beyond search engines. Increasingly, disciplines—from sociology to economics, from the arts to literature—are in search of media as a way to revitalize their methods and objects of study. Our current media situation therefore seems to imply a new term, understood as temporal shifts of mediatic conditioning. Most broadly, then, this series asks: What are the terms or conditions of knowledge itself?

To answer this question, each book features interventions by two (or more) authors, whose approach to a term—to begin with: *communication, pattern discrimination, markets, remain, machine, archives, organize, action at a distance*—diverge and converge in surprising ways. By pairing up scholars from North America and Europe, this series also advances media theory by obviating the proverbial "ten year gap" that exists across language barriers due to the vagaries of translation and local academic customs and in order to provoke new descriptions, prescriptions, and hypotheses—to rethink and reimagine what media can and must do.

Introduction

Studies in Disconnection: On the Fringes of COVID-19

Tero Karppi

There is a certain sense of strangeness to write the introduction to a book on *undoing networks* in voluntary self-isolation.[1] The once open and connected world is suddenly disconnected and physically more separated than ever before. National borders are being closed, international travel is banned, people are encouraged—or sometimes forced with the threat of a fine—to seek shelter or stay home, employers are moving work to internet platforms to avoid physical meetings, and many universities around the world have transitioned from teaching in-person classes to online environments. The cause of this situation in the spring of 2020, as might go without saying, is the outbreak of the coronavirus COVID-19, whose symptoms include dry cough, shortness of breath, fever, and even deathly pneumonia.[2] While the mortality rate estimates differ from source to source and country to country, emergency measures are being put in place at local, regional, national, and global scales to help healthcare systems cope with the outbreak. First identified in the Wuhan area of China in December 2019, the novel coronavirus quickly went global. To anyone for whom virality had become associated with social media and a certain business logic where "money" follows "social influence as it spreads across a network" (Sampson 2012, 2), COVID-19 provides a timely reminder about the epidemiological traces of virality. The rapid spread of the virus shows that networks, whether physical or virtual, can give rise to an uncontrolled, wild, and even destructive form of connectivity. "[N]etworks," as Alexander Galloway and Eugene Thacker (2007, 6) point out, sometimes "carry with them the most nonhuman and misanthropic tendencies." By March 11, COVID-19 was recognized as a pandemic by the World Health Organization. Due to the rapid spread of the virus, disconnection, evasion, isolation, and avoidance became the new social norm, and online connections the preferred mode of social interaction. While we may be done with physical network*ing* (at least for a while), we are not done with networks. In fact, as a form of "biological network," "emerging infectious diseases . . . are highly dependent on one or more networks" (Galloway and Thacker 2007, 90). The virus spreads within networks, and network models are used to explain how COVID-19 becomes contagious; epidemiology and machine learning attempt to model and anticipate its movements. If virality thrives within networks, predicting the edges and cutting the nodes can be a way to bring it under control.

The control of networks and our personal connectivity with them has been one of the key topics of the recent scholarly discussion on the practices and theories of disconnection. The emergence of this nascent field we call here *disconnection studies* is conjoined with the rise of social media and other technological platforms of networked connectivity that have normalized the digital (Kuntsman and Miyake 2019, 902). The "intensification of attention economy," the political push toward digitalization of societies and their services, together with trends like self-optimization have been discussed as reasons individuals begin to challenge the premises of ubiquitous connectivity (Syvertsen 2020, 7–8). Studies of disconnection pay attention to users' practices of resistance against particular digital platforms (Light 2014; Brennen 2019) but also criticize, for example, the principles of digital capitalism and exploitative data practices underlying the existing social network models

(Bucher 2020; Natale and Treré 2020; Karppi 2018). The vectors of disconnection studies constitute different methodological practices dedicated to exploring the individual and collective tactics and strategies of living with networks from empirical research to media art and research creation, and find inspiration in the media-theoretical underpinnings of failures, breaks, disruptions, and states of exception.

Disconnection studies approach notions such as connectivity and practices like networking from a direction where the interest is not in the unity they create but quite on the contrary. "The word 'disconnection' is a verb and implies the removal or breaking a connection," writes Ben Light (2014, 150) in the first book-length study of online disconnection. Breaks, disruptions, and removals turn our attention to the meaning of making connections and the significance of connectivity (Sundén and Blagojević 2019, 57), as well as to the fact that disconnection cannot exist without connections (Hesselberth 2018). The flipside of Pepita Hesselberth's "paradox of disconnection" is of course also true: there is no connection without the potentiality of disconnection (Hesselberth 2018; Light and Cassidy 2014). Connections are always fragile and need to be sustained, maintained, and managed (Strathern 1996, 523; Karppi 2018).

As Gilles Deleuze (1989, 280) famously defined, theory is "a practice of concepts" that interferes with other concepts coming from different practices. The studies of disconnection come with an arsenal of different concepts such as unplugging, unfriending, and withdrawal; these studies unpack devices like Faraday cages, dwell into meetings that take place in detox camps, examine practices of digital minimalism, and ask if digital suicide can really end the life of a data double (for the discussion of these notions see chapter 4). In this book, the concept of *undoing* provides the optics for looking at disconnection. As part of the disconnection vocabulary, *undoing* is a notion that highlights activity. In his book on radical empiricism, William James (1912, 161) writes that "any apprehension of something *doing,* is an experience of activity." For James, doing is a form of bare activity and "the sense of 'life'" is constituted by the experience of changes taking place (James 1912, 161). Something doing indicates activity, and without activity there is nothing (Massumi 2011, 1). Erin Manning (2015, 55) argues that "when something does, new relational fields are forming, and with them, new modes of existence." Undoing is not the negation of doing but a more specified activity where the change taking place is often evoked as resistance (Deutsch 2007, 122). The dictionary definition of "undo," for example, is to untie, unfasten, or loosen, and it can indicate a process of canceling or reversing results. Undoing uses the power of what Karen Barad (2007, 175) has called an "agential cut"—a temporal separation that reconfigures parts in an assemblage. The impacts of undoing range from responsive to critical and even to the extreme of destructive.

The project of this book is to examine and even draw such cuts, to undo what different connections and network models are doing to our experiences, and to ask how networks appear when approached from angles that challenge and reverse the constitutive order of the past two decades: *to connect*. The intention of the following passages of this introductory essay is to think some of the core ideas of disconnection studies by reflecting what the COVID-19 has done to our tendencies to connect. As pointed out by Adi Kuntsman and Esperanza Miyake (2018, 903–4), studies of digital disengagement too often conflate the social with the digital. The pandemic forces us to revise and undo some of the ties that bind these two notions together.

Let us thus begin *in medias res,* by mapping the specificities of this situation as it is unfolding in spring 2020. First of all, the pandemic makes clear that disconnection is not an exclusively online phenomenon (Light 2014; see chapter 1 in this book). Since the virus spreads through any physical network consisting of humans, the only way to slow it down and prevent it from affecting at-risk populations is to cut off all physical contact. Children are not supposed to meet their grandparents; the sick are supposed to remain indoors. Practices like quarantine and self-isolation disrupt our daily practices and force us to determine which connections are really necessary, which may be disregarded, and which should be avoided completely. "Connection and disconnection are dynamic processes that are constantly under re-negotiation," as Anne Kaun and Christian Schwarzenegger (2014) argue.

Studying disconnection means exploring and theorizing how to think both with and beyond the dominant imaginaries of connectivity. If connectivity is about putting things to work by mobilizing the "forms, dynamics, and spatial parameter of operations," then disconnection is expressed in the forms of "stillness, waiting, and de-intensification" (Tellmann, Opitz, and Stäheli 2012, 210–11). When networks fail, we are left balancing between a sense of "helplessness and the desire for control" (Paasonen 2014, 703). In April 2020, many basic services have been reduced, air travel is possible only in special circumstances, no one knows when daycares and schools will reopen. Goods still move but people remain in place. The virus has driven financial markets into a state of crisis. We can only wait in this disconnected state.

We are all in this together, as politicians, the press, and experts declare, but our positions are hardly equal. Disconnection studies raise questions about the capital, labor, and knowledge needed to withdraw. While networking has long been a central skill in many professions, only the introvert seems to thrive in social isolation (see chapter 1 in this book). The ability to disconnect demands social capital in the form of networks that exist outside social media (Portwood-Stacer 2013), particular skills (Syvertsen 2018), knowledge (Kaun and Treré 2018), and is sometimes a luxury of the few and reflective of their positions of power (Karppi and Nieborg 2020).

In the pandemic, working from home is encouraged, though not everyone has this privilege. Among the first to feel the impact of the recession were the airlines, whose job had been to connect people, countries, and continents. Essential workers, such as health care workers and first responders, cannot work from home.

"Long-standing systemic health and social inequities have put some members of racial and ethnic minority groups at increased risk of getting COVID-19 or experiencing severe illness, regardless of age," research by Centers of Disease Control and Prevention (2020) in the United States shows. People with lower income and for example new immigrants are being affected by the pandemic more adversely (CBC News 2020). Those whose income depends on the new gig economy cannot withdraw; they keep bringing food and goods to people who order them online from the relative safety of isolation.

In the virus era, whether biological or computer-based, everyone is made responsible for not only keeping themselves safe but also ensuring the safety of others (Parikka 2007). Practices of disconnection render self-regulation visible and make it normative (Jorge 2019). A prime example of the new normal associated with disconnection is the practice of "social distancing." "Put simply," the *New York Times* explains, "the idea is to maintain a distance between you and other people—in this case, at least six feet. That also means minimizing contact with people. Avoid public transportation whenever possible, limit nonessential travel, work from home and skip social gatherings—and definitely do not go to crowded bars and sporting arenas" (Mandavilli 2020). A sign on the gate of a closed public park in Toronto, Canada, declares: "Practice good physical distancing—two metres apart or about the length of a hockey stick." Keeping the distance of a hockey stick protects people, because COVID-19 spreads via respiratory droplets produced from coughing or sneezing. The practice of social distancing has become one of the key symbols of the preventive measures governments, organizations, and individuals are taking against the threat of COVID-19 infection. Other symbols include face masks (see also chapter 2 on privacy wear), hand sanitizers, and toilet paper, which quickly sold out or moved to the black market. People in masks now appear everywhere in public—in airports, schools, parks, and restaurants—if they are not closed already.

Social distancing, self-isolation, quarantine, and states of exception have only intensified what Gilles Deleuze once defined as the old modes of control, associating them with Michel Foucault's notion of disciplinary mechanisms. We are witnessing the revival of techniques of enclosure that are based on spatial partitioning and physically separating people from each other (Deleuze 1992; Foucault 1979, 195–200). Different guidelines continue to be implemented by nation-states in order to "flatten the curve" and ensure that each of their own health care systems can manage its patients. To slow down the spread of the virus, anyone who has been in touch with an infected individual or has traveled in high-risk areas is asked or forced to self-isolate for fourteen days. Those who exhibit signs of infection are placed in quarantine.

Disconnection constitutes not only a break but "also a state in which something can exist in" (Light 2014, 150). Social distancing, quarantine, and self-isolation all protect us from the virus. Among other countries, Finland declared a state of emergency, which granted juridical rights to limit the size of any meetings—first to no more than five hundred and soon to no more than ten participants. New rules and restrictions go into effect every day. Restaurants offer only takeout. Gyms, hairdressers, beaches, and many other public spaces are forced to close indefinitely. Being "corona free" is now a selling point on Tinder. Individuals are voluntarily carving out their own isolated zones where new social norms apply: no hugging, no touching, no forms of physical contact. In the pandemic, life itself is being protected by disconnection.

Nation-states try different tactics to control the pandemic, from nudging the citizens' social behavior toward more socially distant interactions to closing the borders to noncitizens (see also chapter 3 on nudging). One critic of the exceptional measures taken by certain nation-states is Giorgio Agamben (2020a; 2020b). In response, Jean-Luc Nancy points out that "exception" is not an anomaly but is "becoming the rule in a world where technical interconnections of all kinds (movement, transfers of every type, impregnation or spread of substances, and so on) are reaching a hitherto unknown intensity that is growing at the same rate as the population," and the role of the government is just one small piece of the puzzle (Nancy 2020).

When Foucault wrote about the exceptional measures taken to control the plague at the end of the seventeenth century, by separating contaminated spaces and people from those perceived to be healthy, he also highlighted the role of practices such as classifying, registering, and reporting that emerged alongside (Foucault 1979, 196–97). Virus discourses, both biological and computational, that focus on the threats and vulnerabilities subsisting in connection seem inseparable from the practices that shaped the network culture in the 1990s (Parikka 2007, 94–96; McKinney and Mulvin 2019). Similarly, the responses to Covid-19 are accompanied by a development of new digital practices designed to control the risk of contamination. Mark Andrejevic and Neil Selwyn describe "how smartphones can be repurposed as monitoring systems to support the management and control of the public," for instance, by forcing everyone to download an app that lets individuals know whether they can leave their apartments (Andrejevic and Selwyn 2020). In Germany, Deutsche Telekom is giving out smartphone location data for tracking the movements of the general public and making predictions about the spread of the virus (Schaer 2020). In May, Apple and Google introduced an automated "contact tracing" system where smartphones via Bluetooth connect automatically with other phones in proximity.[3] The recorded information about the time and space of contact can then be used to warn the owners of the possible exposure to the virus. If social networks were based on establishing digital connections for users to stay in touch with their existing networks of friends, colleagues, or people they share interests with, regardless of their physical time and location, COVID-19 brings forward its reverse image. In the new world, the social is determined by the digital, which undoes physical social networks by dictating when, where, and with whom you can stay in touch and who are to be isolated from their peers.

COVID-19 is a variation of a "corona" virus, which was given this name because its shape exhibits a fringe projection resembling the rarefied gaseous envelope of the sun or other stars. In the pandemic era, physical connections are precisely the ones that are rarefied, and disconnection is no longer a fringe projection. While techniques of social distancing may succeed in physically isolating people from their offline environments, isolation does not necessarily extend to online spaces. Quite the contrary, many daily practices that used to happen face-to-face, from meetings to teaching and doctor's appointments, are now being moved online. From playdates to after-work meetings, people are forging new social relations online. Those who left Facebook now consider returning in order to find a sense of community in self-isolation. Teleconferencing apps like Zoom, Skype, and FaceTime have taken on renewed significance. Newer social networks like Nextdoor are becoming places where people can seek and offer local help. For many, disconnecting from physical social circles amplifies the importance of their online counterparts.

In quarantine, social life plays out primarily online, where "social distancing" is a misnomer. In recent years, internet researchers have repeatedly shown that online connections can be very real and personal, and that physical distance in an era of digital media no longer amounts to social isolation (Baym 2010). In fact, the concept preferred over "social distancing" by experts such as the World Health Organization is "physical distancing," since the clear spatial order of the latter is more descriptive than the vague symbolism of the former. In a pandemic, physical disconnection becomes a pragmatic state of life itself.

When Alexander Galloway and Eugene Thacker were writing about networks more than a decade ago, they were demanding that we account for the unhuman aspects of these networks. We are no longer in control of even our own networks. With their emphasis on the unhuman side of the networks, Galloway and Thacker turn our attention to the "materiality of networks," which "exhibits power relations regardless of powerful individuals" (2007, 153). Their central argument is that the understanding of networks, especially digital ones, has been too human-centric, which leads scholars to neglect how network infrastructure, exemplified by protocols, establishes the very conditions for directing and distributing human action.

These claims have been developed and nuanced by software and platform studies, which have tended to invest in decentering the human from network analysis. Today, the unhumanity of networks is expressed by the uncontrollability of biological viruses and how, from the perspective of the virus, human bodies, human touch, and even human connection are nothing more than an exploitable structure in a contagious network.

Galloway and Thacker point out that "networks operate through ceaseless connections and disconnections . . . They are forever incomplete but always take on a shape" (2007, 156). When the humans are decentered from the physical proximity from each other, the power of the social takes other shapes. One place where the undone offline networks release their social power is online networks and different technologies of the social. Our physical social networks, however, do not just move from one environment to another, and social is not conflated with the digital without consequence. Just like in the offline world, also in the online world life shapes and is shaped by the networks where it happens. The problem is that digital networks are not merely unhuman but sometimes also inhuman. Once seen as an embodiment of participatory democracy, many digital platforms have become networks for fake news, hate speech, and "offer the most destructive forces an ideal propaganda system" (Vaidhyanathan 2018, 195). The revenue of these platforms is based on exploiting not only users' private information but also their behavioral patterns. Social media platforms actively define "what it means to be social, and what they think should be filtered out as anti-social" (Carmi 2020, 121). "Overconnection" has become recognized as a real problem (Baym et al. 2020). While digital networks are clearly exploitative of human value and draw new definitions for human capital, we are pushed even more deeply into them, in the era of COVID-19, rather than disconnected from them. What used to be conceived as overconnection becomes the default.

Before a vaccine is developed, the disciplinary mechanisms of disconnection are targeted toward networks; many of them are methods of cutting links between the nodes, isolating individuals into smaller subsets that are easier to control. Simultaneously, jobs, education, and our personal relationships move from in-person meetings to online networks. This is a moment where we need studies of disconnection to make visible the in- and unhuman relations different networks make possible. But even more importantly, when the links are being cut, physical networks undone, and offline becomes substituted with the online, how to take care for each individual node becomes a question that needs to be addressed by these same studies. While Galloway and Thacker once encouraged us not to define digital networks from human-centric perspectives—because the human, by default, is not a central concern of these networks—human-centric perspectives are the very ones we now need.

||||||||||||||||

Undoing Networks is an attempt to examine what it means to be *in disconnection*. What is the experience of being in the middle of things that break, disrupt, unfasten, and cut. In disconnection, we are faced with the activity of drawing the limits of a network and setting its boundaries. Internet celebrities are burning out, individuals are visiting digital detox camps, policymakers are imagining how to restrict social platforms, and people seem to be more conscious of their privacy. If the first two decades of this new millennium were about establishing different forms of connectivity from the birth of social media to algorithmic recommendation systems and the rise of the figure of the influencer, we are only now coming to terms with the wider cultural and political implications of this change. The downfall of the major social platforms and network models these firms have incorporated in their business strategies and of which they have been benefitting from for two decades is perhaps not here yet. But it feels closer than before.

In disconnection, one is neither with nor against the networks but always somewhere in between. As Clara Wieghorst and Lea P. Zierott note in the opening to chapter 4, "disconnection is embedded in our everyday lives." With its structure, this book tries to capture this embeddedness and show how our culture of ubiquitous connectivity can be challenged and its fundamentals criticized and denaturalized from within. This introduction included, the book is built around five distinct components that are disconnected from each other methodologically and practically. The first chapter seeks for the role of the human in network theory from classical sociological texts to the emergence of 5G networks. The second and fourth chapters diverge from more traditional scholarly takes. The former interviews a fashion designer whose clothes are not for visibility but for privacy. The latter adopts the keywords format to articulate some of the nodes and edges in the network of disconnection studies. The third chapter undoes Facebook's privacy proposition with a close reading of a technical feature. To follow the logic of undoing, the chapters invite the reader to a continuous process of connecting, disconnecting, and reconnecting.

In the first chapter, Urs Stäheli argues that we need to understand the genealogy of connectivity both within and beyond the digital. As a first step toward a sociology of undoing networks, Stäheli traces disconnection back to the works of sociologists Georg Simmel and Gabriel Tarde from around 1900. For Stäheli, these early forms of criticism of networking operate as performative concepts that produce the ways in which we now understand connectivities and disconnectivities. In other words, notions like hyperconnectivity (the possibility of overnetworking), figures of the shy or introverted type (networking is too much), and the condition of schizophrenia (everything is connected) each produce an understanding of connectivity that exceeds its technical aspects. With each of these seemingly individualized figures, however, Stäheli does not argue that disconnection is a subjective problem that can be cured with detoxes or self-care. Rather, he shows that problems of disconnection are part of the imaginaries of network culture; rather than being a mere corollary of connection, disconnection is thus productive as such. This approach allows Stäheli to rework the idea of disconnection—not as complete abstention from technologies of connectivity but as a strategic-tactical in-between area where new techniques and technologies can be designed and created.

Undoing appears in different forms. The work of engineers, activists, artists, and even entrepreneurs who design privacy tools, detox camps, and getting-things-done applications (Draper 2019; Fish 2017; Gregg 2018; Brunton and Nissenbaum 2015) provide insights on the cultural techniques of isolation, distancing, and obfuscation. In the second chapter of this book Lea P. Zierott interviews fashion designer Nicole Scheller, who designs antisurveillance clothes dedicated to concealing one's identity. For Scheller, clothes are the only way to shield an individual's privacy against the already-omnipresent cameras that now connect to ubiquitous recognition systems. For example, she works with a coating that reflects infrared light and knits pullovers with patterns that obstruct algorithmic recognition systems. Scheller makes visible the process that renders individuals legible to technology and makes them part of the discourses of connectivity. The interview highlights that conscious undoing demands activity and posits the importance of considering a maker's perspective based on concrete materiality on disconnection.

In the third chapter, Tero Karppi explores Facebook's "Off-Facebook Activity" privacy tool, which is designed to give individuals control over what information flows between Facebook and particular advertisers. "The best person to be in control of data is you," declare the makers of the tool (Facebook 2020). But rather than empowering the users from the inside, Karppi argues, the very existence of the tool and its discourses serves to constitute a specific outside. Disconnection, in this case, means working on building boundaries and determining what Facebook is and what the limits of connectivity are. By doing a close reading of the promotional materials for the Off-Facebook Activity tool, Karppi maps how the tool draws technical borders between the Facebook platform, its users, and advertisers by disconnecting the links between them. Karppi also analyzes how the discourses around the tool nudge users toward particular forms of exteriority. In other words, when the Off-Facebook Activity tool defines Facebook's outside, it not only puts this definition into practice as a function of technology but also weaves it into the surrounding discourses. The limits of what lies outside networks are at once technical, social, and psychological.

The concluding section of the book aims to open new areas for studies of disconnection by ratifying some of the concepts and phenomena where disconnection currently takes form. To this end, a glossary by Clara Wieghorst and Lea P. Zierott maps the discourse networks where disconnection currently appears, is examined, or should be. The keywords they explore range from specific empirical cases, such as *dead zones,* the *right to disconnect,* and the meaning of *offline,* to more general concepts, such as *unfriending, unfollowing,* and *unplugging.* The glossary as a whole illustrates that disconnection is never monolithic and, whether we like it or not, we are now confronted with a radically different imaginary where future belongs to disconnection.

"There is much more to be learned from practice, from *doing,*" Finn Brunton and Helen Nissenbaum (2015) maintain when writing about the different tactics and practices applied to protect privacy. Similarly, we hope to show that there is much to be learned from *undoing*—an activity where resistance makes sense to life and keeps the processes of the world open for something new. As this book shows, undoing is a complex practice. In fact, it is composed of different "disconnective practices" (Light 2014) that can untie the knots of connectivity, from detoxes to countersurveillance measures, from bans of technology to their failure. Each practice is unique and their research asks for methodologies dedicated to unpacking and deconstructing the elements that compose those networks, from technical features to the discourse networks that surround them. To undo is to bring down the dogmatic theories of connectivity according to which the elements of a network are conjoined, for example, by showing how the dominant network theories of the social are based on particular understandings of subjectivity, or asking who is benefitting from the modes of sociality current digital platforms make possible. Undoing networks underlines the fact that connectivity, especially in its digital forms, is artificially created, follows particular understandings of what a network is and who the users are, and is established for specific purposes. *Undoing Networks* is a call to think beyond the connected status of our current situation.

Notes

1 This introduction was written during the first wave of the pandemic. It maps how the situation developed in the spring of 2020.

2 Writing a book is always a collective effort. On behalf of myself and the other authors of this book, I would like to express our gratitude to Timon Beyes for his help with managing the entire process; Melissa Gregg and Finn Brunton for providing valuable feedback; Erik Born for translations, copyediting, and feedback; and Inga Luchs for helping us with formatting the chapters.

3 See https://covid19.apple.com/contacttracing.

References

Agamben, Giorgio. 2020a. "The Invention of an Epidemic." *European Journal of Psychoanalysis*, February 26. Accessed April 27, 2020. https://www.journal-psychoanalysis.eu/coronavirus-and-philosophers/.

Agamben, Giorgio. 2020b. "Clarifications." *An und für sich*, March 17. Accessed April 22, 2020. https://itself.blog/2020/03/17/giorgio-agamben-clarifications/.

Andrejevic, Mark, and Neil Selwyn. 2020. "The New Transparency: Smartphones, Data Tracking, and COVID-19." *Lens*, March 9. Accessed April 2020. https://lens.monash.edu/2020/03/09/1379796/the-new-transparency-smartphones-data-tracking-and-covid-19.

Barad, Karen. 2007. *Meeting the Universe Halfway: Quantum Physics and the Entanglement of Matter and Meaning.* Durham, N.C.: Duke University Press.

Baym, Nancy K. 2010. *Personal Connections in the Digital Age.* Cambridge, Mass.: Polity.

Baym, Nancy K., Kelly B. Wagman, and Christopher J. Presaud. 2020. "Mindfully Scrolling: Rethinking Facebook after Time Deactivated." *Social Media + Society* 6, no.2: 1–10.

Brennen, Bonnie. 2019. *Opting Out of Digital Media.* New York: Routledge.

Brunton, Finn, and Helen Nissenbaum. 2015. *Obfuscation: A User's Guide for Privacy and Protest.* Cambridge, Mass.: MIT Press.

Bucher, Taina. 2020. "Nothing to Disconnect From? Being Singular Plural in an Age of Machine Learning." *Media, Culture & Society* 42, no. 4: 610–17.

Carmi, Elinor. 2020. "Rhythmedia: A Study of Facebook Immune System." *Theory, Culture & Society* 37, no. 5:119–38.

CBC News. 2020. "Lower Income People, New Immigrants at Higher COVID-19 Risk in

Toronto, Data Suggests." May 12. Accessed July 9, 2020. https://www.cbc.ca/news/canada/toronto/low-income-immigrants-covid-19-infection-1.5566384.

Centers of Disease Control and Prevention. 2020. "COVID-19 in Racial and Ethnic Minority Groups." Updated June 25. Accessed July 9, 2020. https://www.cdc.gov/coronavirus/2019-ncov/need-extra-precautions/racial-ethnic-minorities.html.

Deleuze, Gilles. 1989. *Cinema 2: The Time-Image.* Minneapolis: University of Minnesota Press.

Deleuze, Gilles. 1992. "Postscript on the Societies of Control." *October* 59: 3–7.

Deutsch, Francine M. 2007. "Undoing Gender." *Gender & Society* 21, no. 1: 106–27.

Draper, Nora. 2019. *The Identity Trade: Selling Privacy and Reputation Online*. New York: New York University Press.

Facebook. 2020. "Off-Facebook Activity." Accessed April 22, 2020. https://www.facebook.com/off-facebook-activity.

Fish, Adam. 2017. "Technology Retreats and the Politics of Social Media." *Triple-C* 15, no. 1. Accessed April 22, 2020. https://doi.org/10.31269/triplec.v15i1.807.

Foucault, Michel. 1979. *Discipline and Punish*. New York: Vintage Books.

Galloway, Alexander, and Eugene Thacker. 2007. *The Exploit: A Theory of Networks*. Minneapolis: University of Minnesota Press.

Gregg, Melissa. 2018. *Counterproductive: Time Management in the Knowledge Economy*. Durham, N.C.: Duke University Press.

Hesselberth, Pepita. 2018. "Discourses on Disconnectivity and the Right to Disconnect." *New Media & Society* 20, no. 5: 1994–2010.

James, William. 1912. *Essays in Radical Empiricism.* New York: Longmans, Green & Co.

Jorge, Ana. 2019. "Social Media, Interrupted: Users Recounting Temporary Disconnection on Instagram." *Social Media + Society.* October: 1–19.

Karppi, Tero. 2018. *Disconnect: Facebook's Affective Bonds.* Minneapolis: University of Minnesota Press.

Karppi, Tero, and David B. Nieborg. 2020. "Facebook Confessions: Corporate Abdication and Silicon Valley Dystopianism." *New Media & Society.* June 29. doi:10.1177/1461444820933549.

Kaun, Anne, and Christian Schwarzenegger. 2014. "'No Media, Less Life?' Online Disconnection in Mediatized Worlds." *First Monday* 19, no. 11. Accessed April 22, 2020. https://firstmonday.org/ojs/index.php/fm/article/view/5497.

Kaun, Anne, and Emiliano Treré. 2018. "Repression, Resistance, and Lifestyle: Charting (Dis)connection and Activism in Times of Accelerated Capitalism." *Social Movement Studies,* December 12. Accessed April 22, 2020. https://doi.org/10.1080/14742837.2018.1555752.

Kuntsman, Adi, and Esperanza Miyake. 2019. "The Paradox and Continuum of Digital Disengagement: Denaturalising Digital Sociality and Technological Connectivity." *Media, Culture & Society* 41, no. 6: 901–13.

Light, Ben. 2014. *Disconnecting with Social Networking Sites.* London: Palgrave MacMillan.

Light, Ben, and Elijah Cassidy. 2014. "Strategies for the Suspension and Prevention of Connection: Rendering Disconnection as Socioeconomic Lubricant with Facebook." *New Media & Society* 16, no. 7: 1169–84.

Mandavilli, Apoorva. 2020. "Wondering about Social Distancing?" *The New York Times*, March 16. Accessed April 22, 2020. https://www.nytimes.com/2020/03/16/smarter-living/coronavirus-social-distancing.html.

Manning, Erin. 2015. "Against Method." In *Non-Representational Methodologies: Re-Envisioning Research*, ed. Phillip Vannini, 51–71. New York: Routledge.

Massumi, Brian. 2011. *Semblance and Event: Activist Philosophy and the Occurrent Arts*. Cambridge, Mass.: MIT Press.

McKinney, Cait, and Dylan Mulvin. 2019. "Bugs: Rethinking the History of Computing." *Communication, Culture & Critique* 12: 476–98.

Nancy, Jean-Luc. 2020. "Viral Exception." *European Journal of Psychoanalysis*, February 27. Accessed April 27, 2020. https://www.journal-psychoanalysis.eu/coronavirus-and-philosophers/.

Natale, Simone, and Emiliano Treré. 2020. "Vinyl Won't Save Us: Reframing Disconnection as Engagement." *Media, Culture & Society* 42, no. 4: 626–33.

Paasonen, Susanna. 2015. "As Networks Fail: Affect, Technology, and the Notion of the User." *Television & New Media* 16, no. 8: 701–16.

Parikka, Jussi. 2007. *Digital Contagions: A Media Archaeology of Computer Viruses*. New York: Peter Lang.

Portwood-Stacer, Laura. 2013. "Media Refusal and Conspicuous Non-consumption: The Performative and Political Dimensions of Facebook Abstention." *New Media & Society* 15, no. 7: 1041–57.

Sampson, Tony D. 2012. *Virality: Contagion Theory in the Age of Networks*. Minneapolis: University of Minnesota Press.

Schaer, Cathrin. 2020. "Coronavirus: They Want to Use Your Location Data to Fight Pandemic. That's a Big Privacy Issue." *ZDNet*, March 19. Accessed April 22, 2020. https://www.zdnet.com/article/coronavirus-they-want-to-use-your-location-data-to-fight-pandemic-thats-a-big-privacy-issue/.

Strathern, Marilyn. 1996. "Cutting the Network." *The Journal of the Royal Anthropological Institute* 2, no. 3: 517–35.

Sundén, Jenny, and Jelisaveta Blagojević. 2019. "Dis/connections: Toward an Ontology of Broken Relationality." *Configurations* 27, no. 1: 37–57. Accessed April 22, 2020. doi:10.1353/con.2019.0001.

Syvertsen, Trine. 2018. *Media Resistance: Protest, Dislike, Abstention*. London: Palgrave Macmillan.

Syvertsen, Trine. 2020. *Digital Detox: The Politics of Disconnecting*. Bingley, UK: Emerald Publishing Limited.

Tellmann, Ute, Sven Opitz, and Urs Stäheli. 2012. "Operations of the Global: Explorations of Connectivity." *Distinktion: Journal of Social Theory* 13, no. 3: 209–14.

Vaidhyanathan, Siva. 2018. *Antisocial Media: How Facebook Disconnects Us and Undermines Democracy*. New York: Oxford University Press.

[1]

Undoing Networks

Urs Stäheli

Translated by Erik Born

Only a few years ago, "networking" appeared to be a prophetic buzzword, "making connections" an emancipatory slogan.[1] Hardly any area of culture or society was immune to the demand to network better, which is to say, to make more contacts, strengthen existing ties, and, in the words of one industry's refashioned ABCs, "always be connecting." Networking was supposed to flatten out corporate hierarchies and transform traditional companies into highly interconnected organizations. It provided a virulent image for political movements, which came to understand themselves as flexible, extensible, and modular systems. Networking even found a place in "relational art," which turned audience participation into an interactive aesthetic practice. Digital networking, in particular, was nowhere more celebrated than in early internet discourses, which took making connections to be a means of liberation from once-exclusionary structures. To the technological avant-garde (documented in magazines like the aptly named *Wired*) and critics of Internet culture alike, democratic participation seemed to herald a better and more open future, and a participatory principle appeared to have been hardwired into digital technologies, coded directly into social media platforms.[2]

In retrospect, however, networking appears to have been more of an imposition. Indeed, we are currently witnessing nothing less than the exhaustion of networking—and not only in the enforcement of "social distancing" or the widespread diagnosis of "burnout." While ubiquitous networking is proving to be an exhausting activity for many individuals, it simultaneously creates an ever tighter and more suffocating network of social control. According to Kate Losse, one of the first Facebook employees, an early speechwriter for Mark Zuckerberg, and later a sharp feminist critic of the platform, networking was originally a hopeful aspiration. In a disillusioned retrospective, Losse describes the hippie spirit pervading early social networks, which once had a "moralistic sense of the mission: of connecting people, connecting the world. It's hard to argue with that. What's wrong with connecting people? Nothing, right?" (Kulwin 2018). At the time, the purpose of connecting more and more people (and things) seemed self-evident: It was not only a realization of technical possibilities but also a step toward a better and more open society. Hence, the founders and early developers of social media platforms like Facebook and Twitter were surprised when their original utopia succumbed to the dual logic of surveillance and economization captured in Shoshana Zuboff's analysis of "surveillance capitalism" (2019). Even the radical theorists of digital network cultures have become disillusioned with networking. While the internet was once taken to be a realization of the flexible and antihierarchical structure of the "rhizome," a critical concept adopted from Gilles Deleuze and Félix Guattari's social theory of power from the 1970s, the lofty expectations of digital cultures have fallen far short of the target. One of the leading media theorists of contemporary digital cultures, Alexander Galloway, who at first argued vehemently under a Deleuzian framework, now succinctly demands that we "Forget Deleuze!" (Berry and Galloway 2016). Otherwise, political enthusiasm for the internet comes too easily under the spell of the same control society it criticizes.

Should networking still be separated from these recent developments and thereby salvaged, assuming that it even remains desirable in and of itself? Where does the notion that connectivity is an intrinsic good come from? And how did the act of making connections come to represent an ethical and political duty (most prominently with the figure of the networker whom Boltanski and Chiapello [2007] have identified as key component of a new spirit of capitalism)? These questions are significant in more than one respect: The concept of connectivity not only points to a central foundation of contemporary digital networks but also to the need for a much longer genealogy of connectivity, which cannot be reduced to the digital. Today, the notion of connectivity, the ability to make connections and expand networks, leaves an imprint on nearly every aspect of society, from predigital social contacts to the digital devices required by social networks. While connectivity clearly informs social media platforms like Facebook, Twitter, and Tumblr, it also affects social areas that may initially seem to be "nondigital": the point of making small talk at parties now appears to be making important cultural or economic contacts; the purpose of academic networking events to be creating interdisciplinary conversations among once-isolated disciplines. In these situations, the first virtue of networking appears to be the constant willingness to make new contacts, combined with the corresponding ability to resist the disappointment caused by failed attempts (Boltanski and Chiapello 2007). The principles of networking have assumed an all-encompassing logic in Western societies, contributing to a widespread "fetish of connectivity" (Pedersen 2013). The logic of connectivity goes hand in hand with an entire arsenal of semantics, techniques, and technologies, which turn it into an ethico-political program that is only partly captured by the notion of self-optimization. While the ethos of self-optimization produced the now-familiar figure of "networkers," who work both to maintain their active networks and to improve their ability to make connections, this seemingly subjective figure only condenses and illustrates a different logic that cannot be reduced to any form of subjectivation. In its elemental structure, the ethos of connectivity functions in a nonsubjective manner, since it always refers to the expansion and intensification of networks. "To connect" turns into a moral imperative, addressing human and nonhuman actors alike. Connectivity does not primarily refer to individual experiences, affects, and mental states but to a specific form of the generativity of networks: the becoming self-referential of making connections. It is this logic that the notion of networks presupposes and fosters: to produce connections for connections' sake. Drawing from actor–network theory (ANT), the notion of networks is not reduced to digital networks but always comprises human and nonhuman connections. Thus, my argument is not to juxtapose technological network connectivity with human connectivity. This would only lead to a familiar and nostalgic narrative of media critique that tries to salvage true connections from reified digital connections. Rather, I argue it is necessary to uncover the sociotechnological impositions that go along with the establishment of connectivity as an ethico-political good of its own.

Genealogies of Hyperconnection

As soon as the expansion of networks, the incessant creation of new connections, becomes an end in itself, the perceived excess in the concept of connection gets problematized in terms of "hyperconnection." This also means that the origins of contemporary diagnoses of a crisis in networking cannot be equated with the ongoing digitalization of social life, reducing the idea of networks to a technological idea. In sociological diagnoses of the present, the first traces of hyperconnection already started to appear around 1900. With the notion of the "blasé attitude," Georg Simmel examined how "the metropolitan type . . . develops an organ protecting him against the threatening currents and discrepancies of his external environment which would uproot him" (Simmel 1950, 410). In addition to his diagnosis of a nascent crisis, Simmel's emphasis on the formation of a blasé attitude presents indifference as one of the earliest techniques of undoing networks, albeit still in an individual form. Following its early aestheticization in the figure of the dandy, this indifferent attitude would eventually become one of the most important techniques for navigating digital environments. Recent years have seen increasing reflection on attention and distraction, even talk of an entire "ethics of indifference" (Tonkiss 2003). In these contemporary contexts, "indifference" describes the possibility of navigating networked situations without succumbing to the ethos of connectivity, which also raises a theoretical question that I can only hint at (Stäheli 2020): Can we conceive of co-presence without necessarily understanding it as an interactive relation?[3]

Around 1900, Simmel's contemporary Gabriel Tarde developed his own sociology of imitation, which Bruno Latour reads as a forerunner of actor–network theory and an early account of the social as networked (Latour 2002). At some points, however, Tarde was more critical of his own principle of universal imitation, since a society based on perfect imitation could easily lose its rich sense of innovation and thus its dynamism, eventually becoming monotonous and homogeneous. For Tarde, the expression of this kind of society, which he saw characterized by its medial structures and its ability to generate endless statistical data long before the advent of "digital" society, was the figure of the somnambulist. A perfect medium for channeling imitation, the somnambulist transmits affects, ideas, and practices without any resistance (Tarde 1903, 76). If one is deliberately looking for the limits of Tarde's early analysis of network society, one will immediately come across the somnambulist's counterpart in another embodiment of indifference—the shy, timid, or introverted type. According to Tarde, "timidity is a conscious and, consequently, an incomplete magnetization . . . It is a *nascent* social *state* which accompanies every transition from one society to another" (86; emphasis in the original).[4] Introverts tend to disrupt the otherwise free-flowing channel of imitation because they distrust the very process of networking, constantly worrying that they might make a faux pas. For Tarde, introverts are inadequately socialized and thus remain too resistant, on an individual level, to serve as a perfect transmission medium.

Tarde was hardly alone in his interest in introversion and other forms of deviation from the perceived norms of connectivity. The turn of the century witnessed the development of a wide-ranging sociopsychological discourse of introverts, who were seen as obstacles to social networking situations on account of their reluctance to communicate (Duga 1922). As a result, introversion came to be pathologized, and the inability to socialize in casual situations was turned into a disease to be treated. In a manner of treatment that would eventually become typical of the network society's burn-out cases, widespread figures of disconnection were classified as pathologies, disorders, and accidents, thereby reinforcing the dominant imperatives of connection.

Refusing to participate in the widespread pathologization of introversion, Tarde expressed remarkable sympathy for introverts' perceived inability to make connections, which he even took to contain the contours of a new ability. The "inability" is not simply a deficiency but a competency of its own, which goes along with a set of practices. It is this that I call the undoing of networks: neither a simple negation of networks, nor just unplugging from networks, but practices within networks that question their ethico-political impositions of connectivity. This sympathy is particularly evident in Tarde's subsequent reframing of his sociology of imitation so as to account for that of non-imitation. In the Preface to the Second Edition of *The Laws of Imitation,* Tarde asserts that "the fact of not imitating when there is no contact . . . is merely a *non-social* relation, but the fact of not imitating the neighbor who is in touch with us, puts us upon a footing of really *anti-social* relations with him" (1903, xix; emphasis added). Rather than the mere absence of imitation, non-imitation would constitute an independent social relation, which needs to be distinguished, in turn, from counterimitation. The crucial implication of Tarde's revised sociology is that non-imitation gives rise to a particular mode of existence, which, even in the presence of spatial proximity and social contact, would not imply interactivity. What I call undoing networks inhabits this conceptual space between connectivity and nonconnectivity: the creation and experimenting with practices that are indifferent but not external to networks. While Tarde never elaborated on this nascent theoretical program, it marks the precise point of departure for a sociology of undoing networks, which could be about more than simply leaving networks or attempting to destroy them. Instead, it needs to address the seemingly disconnected forms of coexistence that do not create any social connections in an emphatic sense. At the same time, the sociology of undoing networks needs to treat disconnection as a social phenomenon, which implies fundamental theoretical questions about the limits of relationality and challenges any theory that views relationality as the defining criterion of the social (Stäheli 2020).[5]

The Desire for Real Connection

In comparison to Simmel's and Tarde's radical outlines of connection and disconnection, many contemporary attempts to deal with hyperconnection are bound to be disappointing. In recent years, the most common pattern of argumentation has been to locate the problem not in networking per se but only in its false and reified forms. To salvage some original sense of human connectivity, which is generally assumed to be "good," the common argument preserves and often even strengthens a universalizing anthropology of *homo conexus* (Bay 2011),[6] the same image of the networked human being that has long served to legitimize network companies. Along these lines, José van Dijck (2013) argues that the "culture of connectedness," which once stood for the democratic and participatory hopes placed on the pre-economized internet, has been replaced by an algorithmically controlled "culture of connectivity." Critiques of digital culture, which are especially prominent in Germany given the nation's current skepticism toward technology, make the problems of connection and disconnection sound even easier. Against the cold and virtual feel of the digital, which may appear to create an autonomous, nonhuman space, critics of digital culture stress the perceived warmth of the analog as the only real space for human society. Exemplarily, the title of one German-language guide to contemporary digital society, *Analog ist das neue Bio,* proclaims "the analog" to be "the new organic" (Wilkens 2015). To many critics of digital culture, the analog represents a refuge for cultivating what they assume makes us truly human, from profound emotions to deep conversations. As the last bastion of traditional society, it must be defended by any means necessary, which is nowhere more evident than in the "digital detox" tourism industry. One particularly visible company, Camp Grounded, made a name for itself by organizing disconnection and detoxification camps for adults in particularly beautiful and remote areas of Northern California (Digital Detox® 2020).[7] Their motto: "Disconnect to Reconnect." From detox resorts and disconnection guidebooks to self-care services and management consultancies, the idea of "digital detox" has been imitated globally. Once again, it is striking that the proponents of disconnection do not necessarily criticize the idea of connectivity per se; they even presume one's familiarity with digital networking as a means of paving the way for what they consider to be even more intensive forms of analog networking. Ignoring one's Facebook timeline, refraining from uploading photos to Instagram, perhaps even abstaining entirely from using one's smartphone for a few days—these simple measures are ultimately intended to serve the noble purpose of getting closer to both oneself and others. In the vein of classic cultural criticism, digital technology takes on the role of the only obstacle standing in the way of one's path toward the real and the true (Bollmer 2016).[8]

These utopias of disconnection, which may sound more like dystopias, attempt to draw a neat dividing line between two forms of connectivity: an originary form of normal human connectivity and its later pathological forms that the current rhetoric of "digital detox" revives (Sutton 2017). In the new dietetic and therapeutic regime, the digital is taken to be a toxin, in analogy to sugar, alcohol, or drugs, that needs to be eliminated from the body through disciplined work on the self, with the analog representing a sort of superfood. Apart from assuming a clear-cut distinction between the digital and the analog, which can hardly be maintained, utopias of disconnection also set in motion a perfidious regime of personal responsibility (Jurgenson 2013). Since individuals are taken to be responsible for their own unhealthy networking behaviors, they can be tasked with protecting themselves against digital temptation and developing a more sustainable lifestyle. Describing excessive digital consumption as an addiction serves to moralize individual failing and turn it into something that can be remedied through therapies, self-examination, educational measures, and self-help guides. As a result, the question of networking is ultimately privatized, even if the classic private sphere, which gave rise to liberal notions of self-responsibility in the first place, no longer exists. Hence, individuals are faced with an insoluble problem, insofar as they are supposed to assume responsibility for their own networking activity but without possessing the autonomy of the classic liberal self.

Any analysis of contemporary networking finds itself faced with an equally challenging dilemma, for which there may initially appear to be only two alternatives. Continuing to cool down the once-heated celebration of networking might end up furthering the technocratic project of increasing prosperity and happiness, though it would still remain tied to this social project's original aim of endlessly improving networking. Then there is the equally problematic retreat to an idealized analog world, which frequently smacks of Luddism and is by no means as innocent as it may appear. As a moralizing technology of "responsibilization" (Shamir 2008), disconnection from the digital seeks to immunize itself against any potential criticism through its purported knowledge of realness and authenticity (Portwood-Stacer 2013). In this current impasse, the only thing that analog nostalgists may appear to have in common with digital apologists is deep disdain. However, these two seemingly irreconcilable positions are united on an even deeper level in their shared belief in the power of making "real" connections.

Critiques of connectivity need to deal with this kind of common ground, which can often be found in a belief in the power of connectivity. Grant Bollmer (2016) rightly points out that contemporary network discourses, regardless of whether they are critical or affirmative, tend to presume a certain anthropology of the networked subject, which is often only latent. The constant development of novel networking technologies is predicated on one particular image of human beings: Being human means living in and through relationships; it depends on both the ability and willingness to make connections with others. If one accepts this image of humanity, one would immediately feel an obligation to care for its core aspects and to keep developing and refining technologies of networking the self. The only thing left to argue about would be whether particular networking techniques are "right" or "wrong," "sick" or "healthy," "efficient" or "inefficient"; there would be no arguing about the ironclad principle of connectivity itself. Ultimately, this anthropology of connectivity, which takes the essence of human beings to consist in their ability to cultivate relationships and make connections, reinforces the contemporary imperative to network, whether in digital or analog form.

Network Fever

When I speak of "networks," I am referring to far more than digital interfaces and technical infrastructures. One of the simplest definitions of a network is the links (aka "edges") among various intersections (aka "nodes"), which result in specific patterns of connection. According to this definition, the internet is only one among many networks, which also include companies, circles of friends, mafia-like organizations, transportation infrastructures, and global trade relations. In recent years, this classic conception of networks has been subject to many critiques for presuming the existence of discrete and independent units. One alternative can be found in Latour's actor–network theory, which emphasizes that the nodes defined as "actants" are themselves the result of networking (Latour 2005), thereby shifting our focus to the actual work of networking (i.e., making connections) and making the otherwise static concept of the network dynamic. From this perspective, networks bring together a heterogeneous ensemble of actors and thrive on their own seemingly infinite extensibility, precisely because they no longer have any clear borders. Furthermore, the absence of clear borders allows the ethos of connectivity described above to be embedded into the very structure of the network: the potential to expand ad infinitum becomes a demand to do so. Lastly, this revised view of networking emphasizes that network concepts are not merely descriptive categories; they have their own performative effect and produce the activity of connecting they describe.

Networks are always more than mere descriptive, technical categories. The imperative to connect, thereby expanding the network, feeds on a deep-seated anxiety. Wendy Chun (2006) even describes the internet in terms of its "paranoid" structure. There is never any position outside the network from which it can be seen in full; there is always the danger that parts of the network could fail, that the entire network could get out of control, that connections could be lost or amount to nothing. From the hypothetical perspective of the network itself, there is always a risk that the delicate web might be damaged and that individual components might fail. How do networks react to these deep-seated anxieties, which are not incidental but rather inscribed right into their sociotechnical structure? The answer is simple: with even more networking! Constant surveillance and multilayered controls ensure knowledge of the network's current state. A paranoid network is insatiable. What was once an advantage—being able to expand without much additional effort—quickly becomes part of the problem, as expansion triggers more expansion. Network anxiety may be temporarily calmed by the creation of additional networks but these in turn create more anxiety. Quite appropriately, architecture theorist Mark Wigley (2001) speaks of "network fever."

One main aspect of this contemporary network fever might actually be better described with a concept drawn from early schizophrenia research of the 1950s. According to gestalt psychologist Klaus Conrad, the insatiable desire to make connections is characteristic of the beginning stages of schizophrenia. For the tendency to perceive connections between otherwise unconnected things and events, Conrad coined the term "apophenia" (Conrad 1958). In Conrad's analysis, there is no such thing as coincidence for aphopheniacs: If they miss the tram, they take it to be a sign that some invisible power crossed their path; if a neighbor fails to greet them, they may conclude that this person is working for a secret organization. Always on the search for the unidentified connections responsible for contingent occurrences, apopheniacs end up connecting random events. They are characterized, in Conrad's analysis, by their equally inexhaustible and fantastical desire to make connections and uncover hidden patterns. Conrad's long-forgotten concept of apophenia has witnessed a massive revival with the contemporary study of "big data,"[9] which is another matter of uncovering patterns in seemingly endless amounts of data, only to put them in the service of, let's say, risk analysis and migration control. From apophenia to anxiety, the vocabulary of psychopathology now commonly used to describe network dynamics calls attention to the fact that our current ethos of connectivity was until only very recently still perceived to be something in need of explanation. A certain pathological logic is now inscribed directly into networks—the logic of suspicion, distrust, and uncontrollable intensification, which is simultaneously that of creativity, pattern identification, and making surprising connections.

Hyperconnection is not an accident; it does not befall networks from the outside, does not result merely from the rash and blind propagation of more and more comprehensive systems. What is to blame for hyperconnection is the immanent logic of unlimited growth. Digital technologies make particularly efficient use of this logic by exploiting possibilities that are inherent in network thinking. Networking increasingly is becoming a self-referential process: In unnecessary meetings, distracted managers constantly sneak a peek at their smartphones, only to plan the next equally inconsequential meeting.

For a long time, however, network fever was much less noticeable. If networking can liberate everyone from rigid hierarchies and create new opportunities for access, what problems could there possibly be? Why should anyone be suspicious of the possibility to communicate with more and more people, to connect with more and more things? For their own part, cultural studies and the social sciences have been ill-prepared for the unforeseen crisis of the network society, insofar as they still tend to view networks and other forms of entanglement as forms of liberation from older approaches, which are easy to dismiss as essentialist. Whether in Latour's actor–network theory, which dreams of denser and denser forms of heterogeneous networks, Deleuze's heady celebration of a weed-like rhizome, which linked up with hippie counterculture, or Niklas Luhmann's development of systems theory, which signaled a switch to the much drier notion of connectivity—these perspectives put a premium on making connections and remain fascinated by its seemingly undreamt-of possibilities.

Practices of Undoing Networks

The questions of severing and slowing down connections, of thinning out networks and identifying an excess of connections were long described only in terms of unintentional network malfunctions, which needed to be eliminated whenever possible.[10] In recent years, however, a wide range of fields that originally ridiculed any counterreactions to the dominant ethos of connectivity have started taking them seriously. We are now witnessing the emergence of various practices of undoing networks, which were never accounted for in theory, never factored into the plans with all the network euphoria. Even in the business world, the once-dominant figure of the networker is increasingly subject to competition, as more companies discover the strengths of those employees long accused of lacking the required capacity for teamwork due to their lack of enthusiasm for socializing. In bestsellers like Susan Cain's *Quiet* (2013), introverts are presented as a long-neglected economic resource, since they work more reliably and with greater concentration than talkative networkers.

There have been parallel developments in many other fields. In workplace design, the primary model for a creative workspace was, for a long time, the "open office," which was invented in Quickborn near Hamburg in the 1950s.[11] Now viewed with much greater skepticism, the fate of open offices was eventually tied to that of rapidly spreading "co-working spaces," which led to a veritable loungification of economic life. Hardly satisfied with these changes, many employees today still long for their own office, a closed space that might offer some form of protection against the need to be reachable at all times. In a similar trend, networking was long seen as a guarantee of security for critical infrastructures, since dense military or energy networks could continue to function in the event of a crisis. Today, however, there are increasing calls to take many of these critical infrastructures offline, since they have become vulnerable to cyberattacks in ways that can no longer be controlled (Gaycken and Karger 2011). Some of the most visible techniques of disconnection are prominent among the most connected users: various software providers offer apps that restrict uncontrolled surfing for a limited period of time; signal-blocking cell phone cases are intended to ensure that users are not reachable for a given period of time; bars and restaurants advertise that they offer mobile free zones; vacation hotels are deliberately built in cellular dead zones like the Scottish Highlands; anonymization software promises to make the individual user invisible, untrackable, and thus no longer addressable by the growing surveillance apparatus. The list could go on and on, though it is already clear that the crisis of networking has led to new experiments with undoing networks, which are hardly always successful.

The current engagement with disconnection differs significantly from older fantasies of checking out, encapsulated in the countercultural mantra, "Turn On, Tune In, Drop Out." Undoing networks today does not necessarily mean starting a life outside the network, thereby leaving it completely behind. Even if many current attempts to disconnect are not entirely free from nostalgia for earlier forms of checking out, especially in their own conceptions of themselves, their practices still operate exclusively *within* networks.[12] Undoing networks describes a paradoxical undertaking, which requires using networks to disconnect from networks. Thus, it is not a simple on/off distinction at play here but rather the zone of neither/nor. Undoing networks, thus, does not mean completely withdrawing from networks, nor the naïve idea of turning off the internet (Sprenger 2019). When I speak of "practices of undoing networks," I do not intend to frame them as a subjective problem, as in the popular discourses of digital detox and other forms of self-care. Nor do I intend to claim that there is some absolute state of disconnection. Pitting the overworked individual against the inexorable structure of the network would create an accurate image only of the underlying logic informing *critiques* of networks, rather than networks themselves. Furthermore, it would not provide many insights into the logic of disconnection, nor would it represent the necessary departure point for a sociology of undoing networks, insofar as it again dredges up the classic opposition between society and the individual. For practices of disconnection, the reference point is neither the individual subject nor the surrounding society but the connecting network. Network fever has made the underlying logic of hyperconnection start to appear more problematic, which has in turn given rise to new practices of undoing networks. Crucially, these new practices reveal that simply leaving networks or switching them off are not viable alternatives but oversimplifications, which fail to acknowledge the simultaneity of connection and disconnection. By "simultaneity," I mean not only the logical conclusion that whenever people connect to one network, they disconnect from another, or that connection goes hand in hand with disconnection. While this perspective runs the risk of making disconnecting into the mere correlative of connecting, neither of which would have any positive characteristics in and of itself, it might also make visible an independent reservoir of practices, technologies, and infrastructures of undoing networks.

These heterogeneous practices of undoing networks are characterized by a certain directionality, insofar as they take the problem of hyperconnectivity as an opportunity to develop alternative practices for creating a state of disconnectivity. Turning hyperconnection into a problem is the first step toward undoing networks. This directionality, or tendency to disconnect, derives more from this network-focused "problematization" (in the Foucauldian sense) than from any individual intentions of the actors involved. I do not intend to claim that the very act of problematizing hyperconnection necessarily produces this trajectory on its own in a quasi-functionalistic manner. My claim is that disconnection is always already inscribed into practices and technologies of hyperconnection as its imaginary dimension. Rather than an underlying ideology or an external symbolic framework for practices, the imaginary dimension of undoing networks constitutes an intrinsic part of these practices.[13] Drawing on Benedict Anderson's concept of "imagined communities" (Anderson 2006),[14] I would argue that there has always been an infrastructural foundation to this imaginary, insofar as it refers to the medial constitution of networking (Langenohl 2019). However, the imaginary dimension of these practices need not primarily suggest a community of the disconnected; rather, it might help sound out the limits of networks and make their experience possible. In this respect, a temporal structure plays a decisive role in the imaginary dimension of these practices, as it does in Sheila Jasanoff's definition of sociotechnical imaginaries on the whole—namely, "collectively held and performed visions of desirable futures (or of resistance against the undesirable)" (2015, 28). Hence, there is no such thing as "pure," "raw," or "given" practices of undoing networks; they are always loaded with hopes, fears, and expectations of the future. For the status of practices as undoing, it is irrelevant whether the imagined futures of disconnection—or of being less connected—are attained, since success or failure are not criteria for deciding whether a practice qualifies as disconnection. It is rather the bounded imaginaries of a state less connected or even disconnected that constitute practices of undoing networks.

Tactics and Strategies of Undoing Networks

The directionality of disconnection practices, which is produced by its imaginary dimension, can be analyzed through a classic distinction that dates back to Michel de Certeau's sociology of everyday life, which was in turn derived from Prussian general and military theorist Karl von Clausewitz—namely, "tactics" and "strategies." For Certeau, tactics are situation-dependent and often cunning practices, which have no particular space of their own: "The space of a tactic is the space of the other . . . It does not have the means to *keep to itself,* at a distance, in a position of withdrawal, foresight, and self-collection" (de Certeau 1984, 37; emphasis in the original). By contrast, strategies create their own space—a permanent one, if possible—from which they can operate in a rational mode. Certeau "call[s] a 'strategy' the calculus of force-relationships which becomes possible when a subject of will and power (a proprietor, an enterprise, a city, a scientific institution) can be isolated from an 'environment'" (xix). In this respect, we can draw a preliminary distinction between tactics and strategies of undoing networks. Operating on networks without any sovereign space of their own, tactics of undoing networks do not assume an exhausted but resilient subject. Furthermore, they are not about creatively appropriating network resources or establishing alternatives and carrying out disruptive media campaigns, as in discussions of "tactical media." Rather, tactics of undoing networks exploit moments, such as partial network failure, when weaknesses appear in the imperative to connect itself (Mannell 2017, 44); when the imperative to connect appears particularly grotesque, they can even undermine it and thereby organize non-addressability. In contrast to the euphoric reception of Certeau in the spirit of participatory media and the DIY movement, undoing networks is more about tactics of incommunicability.

At the same time, we also need to modify Certeau's concept of strategy for disconnection. There may be a space for strategies of undoing networks—for instance, in businesses that develop their own strategies for dealing with burnout and a perceived lack of efficiency. But they also have an imaginary dimension, and one of their most immediate effects is to insinuate and create a discursive unit that is supposed to be capable of precisely this kind of strategic action. One might speak here of an imaginary "misrecognition" (in an almost classic psychoanalytic sense). However, we also need to take the functionality of these strategies seriously, since they structure an important part of how we both speak about disconnection and act on it (McKinlay et al. 2009). What is decisive for disconnection strategies is that they formulate their imaginary in close range to functionalistic concepts and tend to frame hyperconnection as a solvable problem. For instance, a company may find that too much time is being spent on meetings and thus attempt to optimize its schedule with mapping software, thereby turning disconnection into a clearly workable problem with a measurable outcome—in this case, reducing the number of hours spent on meetings. From scholarship on the sociology of organizations, however, we know that corporate strategies hardly ever work, at least not for what they hope for. Nevertheless, companies continue to develop these strategies, especially for the problem of disconnection. It is therefore crucial to take the form of strategic formulations seriously without assuming that they will necessarily result in the intended outcome.

Another immediate effect of these strategies is to commodify disconnection by constructing it as a consumable but reliable "experience" (Pine and Gilmore 2011). In this respect, it is worth emphasizing that the nascent disconnection industry, from disconnection guides through detox resorts to management consulting, was essentially created by the pioneers of network platforms themselves, such as Randy Zuckerberg's efforts to encourage digital unplugging (Zuckerberg 2013) or "Camp Grounded," which was founded by Felix Levy after his Silicon Valley career. According to the network logic of infinite extensibility, social media continue to create new possibilities of connection, while wireless sensors and RFID chips are creating an entire Internet of Things. Even if there appears to be no end in sight for the proliferation and expansion of networks, the disconnected or unnetworked type is increasingly attracting the attention of businesspeople, such as Randi Zuckerberg, who is now developing special detox offers for stressed-out networkers. In an interesting turn of events, disconnection—or, to be precise, ideas about what a disconnected life might look like—is considered not only to be a vast space for new networking projects but also something that can be exploited by the experience economy. One might speak here of a new "landgrab" involving the discovery, treatment, and commodification of the disconnected.

Disconnection strategies make themselves and their images of disconnection highly visible. Claiming to know in advance what a life without networks might look like, they attempt to embed the very disconnection they hope to create into the functional logic of local networks. Whether as a novel luxury experience, a security control for critical infrastructures, or an organizational mechanism governing efficiency and creativity, disconnecting is widely presented as a disciplinary strategy requiring mastery, which again reflects the brave and heroic narratives of blogs and guidebooks. In this respect, disconnection strategies are always strategies of power. They are bound up with the questions of who determines the extent of disconnection and in what manner, which techniques of disconnection are to be deployed, and who has access to which forms of disconnection. When analyzing strategic programs and their corresponding assertions, we should not automatically assume that they will function smoothly, thereby reinforcing their description of themselves. Our analysis also needs to account for changes in sovereignty: The sovereign is still the one who is in a position to make decisions about disconnection, but any clear decision is impossible due to the complex structure of practices and infrastructures involved in any form of disconnection.

While strategies of disconnection are highly visible, their corresponding tactics are largely invisible or inconspicuous. Without their own locus of power, disconnection tactics correspond better to the logic of decentralized and heterogenous networks than to the illusion of sovereignty evident in disconnection strategies. While disconnection tactics are also charged with their own imaginary dimension, moreover, they are supported by a much vaguer sense of what disconnection might look like. In this respect, disconnection tactics do not follow the classic model of strategic thought and action, since they do not formulate a clear problem, nor do they develop systematic techniques and practices to solve it—indeed, they even dispense with the visionary formulation of any achievable end for disconnection. Operating within networks, disconnection tactics often develop experimental and situational forms of incommunicability, imperceptibility, and withdrawal. The figure of the introvert takes on an exemplary role here, insofar as introverts attempt, whether consciously or unconsciously, to withdraw from the demands of communication by making them as imperceptible as possible—ideally, disappearing into the architecture of an inner space. In contrast to the heroism of disconnection strategies, these are tactics of the weak, who often have a better sense of the intricacies of network logic than do any elaborately designed strategies. The foundation of disconnection tactics is not an exaggerated sovereign ability to disconnect but what one might call, adapting the sociological concept of "connectivity," "disconnectivity." In contrast to the sociological concept of connectivity (Anschlussfähigkeit, i.e. the ability to connect), disconnectivity stresses the inability to connect (Anschluss*un*fähigkeit).[15] This inability itself is, however, in contrast to the classical concept: not a deficiency, not something that just happens, but an often invisible ability of its own—a nonsovereign undoing of networks. That is also why the humanist anthropology of the naturally connected subject fails in providing critical perspectives on network cultures, since it shares and legitimizes their ethos of connectivity. In my discussion of early sociological ideas of network societies I've emphasized precisely these moments of turning away from the imperative to connect such as the figure of the introvert. They are characterized by an inability to make connections, which I do not mean to present as a failing or a deficit, as in the pathologizing discourse, but rather as an ability to be cultivated. Along these lines, Alexander Galloway speaks of "insufficiency" as the foundation for any critique of network society (Galloway and LaRiviere 2017).

Even if their elementary logic makes tactics function quite differently from strategies, they hardly ever occur in a pure and isolated form. The present typology is intended only as a heuristic, which can help us better understand the respective proportions in various mixtures. It might also help clarify their mutual interdependencies, since strategies of undoing networks are often based on the observation and rearticulation of corresponding tactics. Take the crisis of the open-office model, which was introduced above. To deal with the attendant challenges of disconnection and communication, there is now an entire arsenal of tactics of withdrawal, which aim to make one temporarily unavailable. At first, these tactics were seen as technical problems, often related to measures of discipline and control. With the increased criticism of hyperconnectivity, especially the notion of tireless communication among interconnected teams, these kinds of evasive tactics have taken on a new meaning. Instead of disciplining individuals, they now provide the template for new strategies of disconnecting, such as building retreat sites into organizational plans or having mandatory periods of noncommunication. The same trend can be observed in the development of situational tactics into strategies of resistance, such as the massive difficulties accompanying individual attempts to withdraw from social media platforms like Facebook (Karppi 2018). In these cases, artistic projects like the Suicide Machine can make visible the imperative to connect, while also providing technologies of disconnection. Similarly, attempts at anonymization, which may be laborious and often fail, also give rise to anonymization software and strategies of hypertrophy, such as the creation of misleading data sets. Once again, these examples show that any narrative proceeding from the appropriation of tactics to hegemonic strategies is an overly simplistic construction. In many fields, it is precisely the border between tactics and strategies that proves to be a fertile space for experimentation and the emergence of new technologies of undoing networks. Artistic projects often play an important role here, especially those interested in the materiality of disconnection, exemplified by wearables,[16] Faraday cages,[17] and the aesthetics of disappearance.[18] Each of these fields is witnessing the deployment of an interesting tactic, which involves appropriating former military techniques of screening, shielding, or protection and reactivating the tactical moment within military strategies, from the development of special colors and materials to electromagnetic jammers.

Reducing disconnection to a romanticized set of everyday practices of withdrawal would not only lose sight of this extremely productive space between tactics and strategies, it would also reaffirm the political fallacy that equates strategies with power and tactics with resistance. This kind of reading ultimately overlooks the existence of disconnection tactics that are inscribed into hegemonic calculations of power, such as the deployment of tactics of indifference to ignore unpopular individuals and discount entire social groups. Tactics intended to make oneself unavailable are never carried out in a social vacuum: There is an uneven distribution, for instance, of the ability to evade emails and withdraw from other communication demands, which in many companies remain the exclusive privilege of higher management (Jauréguiberry 2014).

The fact that the border between tactics and strategies functions as a critical space for the emergence of new techniques and technologies also shows that disconnection does not necessarily follow a technophobic impulse. Quite the contrary, we are witnessing the emergence of a rich variety of techniques and technologies of undoing networks, which reveal how many conditions underpin the possibility of disconnection. Once again, disconnection never comes about on its own and remains predicated on the ability to create social distance. When I speak of "undoing networks," I mean precisely this intermediate area between tactics and strategies, which cannot be reduced to a mere disturbance, since it produces independent social forms.

Politics of Undoing Networks

Adapting the polemological vocabulary of tactics and strategies to conceptualize undoing networks points to the fact that it can never be discussed in isolation from questions of power, and that it brings about a newly deviant politics of undoing networks. If the ethos of connectivity originally crystallized as a hegemonic principle in the network-shaped control society and was eventually inscribed into nearly every sociotechnical area, the ethos of (dis)connectivity has recently become the scene of entirely new negotiations. Several years ago, the fast-food chain Burger King launched a controversial campaign known as the "Whopper Sacrifice": Anyone who "defriended" ten Facebook friends using a specially created app would receive one free Whopper (Wortham 2009). As for the former friends, the app would automatically notify them that they had been sacrificed for the cost of one-tenth of a burger. Ultimately, the advertising campaign had to be stopped prematurely because Facebook threatened to take legal action. Even if it was hardly intended to be a political campaign, the Whopper Sacrifice made visible the biopolitical order of social media companies and even challenged the seemingly self-evident notions that connections are desirable per se and that networking is always a matter of increasing connectivity.[19] In an almost classic manner, the politics of undoing networks remain centered on disrupting and denaturalizing the ethos of connectivity. Only in this way can we open our eyes to what it might mean—in a variation on Foucault's well-known saying about being governed—to develop an "art of not being connected so much." Accordingly, countless notions of the political that were originally concerned with emancipation have eventually wound up in a crisis, so long as they relied exclusively on visibility and recognition. In the end, is the radical democratic project of leftist populism nothing more than a massive hegemonic networking project? What would disconnection mean for the classic politics of visibility, such as various forms of identity politics that demand the recognition of previously unheard voices? Would disconnection amount to even greater exclusion or could forms of disconnection contribute to inclusion?

Even if the politics of undoing networks toil away at the heart of received doctrines about connectivity, they are always subject to the threat of becoming depoliticized. Of course, the depoliticization of disconnection always follows a hidden political logic of responsibilization. Framing disconnection as an individual practice of self-care makes isolated individuals appear to be responsible for moderating their own network contacts and for protecting their own privacy.

As a result, undoing networks gets embedded in individual forms of control and loses its collective political relevance: the perceived inability to connect and disconnect, to network and de-network in the "right" way gets coded as a personal failing. At the same time, the transformation of disconnection into a social technology that is put in the service of perfect networking threatens to sacrifice its potential as a critique of the imperative to connect. To address this threat, we need to keep examining the fundamental concepts associated with undoing networks and conceive of the problem in terms of practices, technologies, and infrastructures, so as to avoid making the individual subject into the sine qua non of disconnection. A sociology of undoing networks needs to remain abstract in the sense that it focuses on the modulation of connections and is primarily interested in severing connections, fading them out, making them disappear, or letting them amount to nothing.

If there is more to undoing networks than the isolation of everyday practices and the responsibilization of individuals, it might be found in the collective significance of disconnection for the networking process. In this respect, it does not suffice to simply diagnose the general network fever and criticize the imperative to network, since the same critique could also serve as a means of depoliticizing individuals. The "art of not being connected so much" is not a subjective project but a collective struggle, which plays out in networks around the limits of connectivity. In this respect, architecture theorist Malcolm McCullough (2013) speaks of "ambient commons," a critical term for the political economy of attention and distraction in digital environments. Accordingly, we can revise the question of organizing attention—and with it, the proliferation and connectivity of information—into one of creating environments for collective experience. Only by detaching the experience of connectivity from an individualistic perspective can we hope to explore alternative possibilities of "ambient commoning" (Zehle 2014). The public treatment of disconnection will continue to create new zones of social conflict. While the controversial "right to disconnect" (*droit à la déconnexion*) guarantees that

French workers do not need to be reachable in their free time,[20] the German Green Party is pushing for complete network coverage (ZEIT Online 2020), and the creation of 5G networks continues to escalate tensions between China and the United States. From debates about the right to disconnect to field-specific strategies like cell phone bans in schools, disconnection is increasingly becoming a political challenge, especially in terms of its institutionalization. Even more fiercely contested are attempts to disconnect parts of network topologies, such as the regulation of financial markets or the European Union's controversial "link tax." During the COVID-19 pandemic, social distancing and quarantine measures made clear that the control of disconnection is a highly contested terrain. It is even more apparent in these areas than in the desire for self-care and the longing for a life off the grid that undoing networks always comes down to power. In one of the few contributions to network theory that deals with the productive potential of disconnection, Marylin Strathern shows that cutting connections and limiting networks are extremely powerful gestures (Strathern 1996), which might find an ideal foundation of legitimacy in the growing thematization of hyperconnection. These kinds of disconnection strategies might have a sobering effect on critiques of the ethos of connectivity, insofar as they subordinate disconnectivity to the functional requirements of connectivity. But they also need to imagine moments of withdrawal and develop evasive techniques, which might help us reduce connectivity and strive for collective experiences of the disconnected life. In this respect, disconnection implicitly contains moments that suggest a way out of network fever. One of the most important tasks for disconnection tactics, as well as for their sociological analysis, consists in uncovering these socially fertile moments instead of focusing on individual tips and tricks for living without networks. By exposing the materiality of disconnection in its most controlled form, we might ultimately hope to reactivate the tactical moment inherent in strategies, even if this kind of undertaking remains embedded in a seemingly paradoxical politics of visibility. Any sociology of undoing networks will thus oscillate between strategic formulations of what a life without networks might look like and open-ended tactics that derive the meaning of disconnecting from the ever-changing situation itself.

Notes

1 *Translator's Note:* As in English, the German term used in the title of this essay, *Entnetzung* (disconnection, undoing networks) is the antonym for *Vernetzung* (connection, creating networks), though only the latter term and not the former is attested to in the major German-language dictionaries. While the English terms "connection" and "disconnection" may indirectly suggest the sense of "networking," moreover, their German counterparts directly evoke it through the root "*Netz*" (net). In consultation with the author, I translate *Vernetzung* as "networking," "connecting," or "making connections" and "*Entnetzung* as "de-networking," "disconnecting," "cutting connections," and "undoing networks."

2 For an accessible cross-disciplinary overview of social, aesthetic, and political networks, see, among others, Levine 2015, 112–31; for the classic source on the emancipatory power of social media, Shirky 2011; for an overview of early political hopes in the internet, Papacharissi 2002.

3 For a critique of sociological interactionism and a call for analysis of "minor modes," see Jackson and Piette 2015.

4 The following passages on the introvert are based on Urs Stäheli, "Die Angst vor der Gemeinschaft" (2013).

5 For Simmel's conception of indifference with the figure of nobility (*Vornehmheit*), which itself operates at the margins of sociology, see Simmel 2009, 641–65; for further analysis of the role of indifference in Simmel's work, see Stäheli 2018.

6 For a critical perspective, see Llamas and Belk 2013.

7 For a critical perspective, see Sutton 2017; Stäheli and Stoltenberg 2020.

8 For a historical overview, see Hesselberth 2018a.

9 Especially prominent in danah boyd's blog *Apophenia* (2004), which turns the pathological semantics of apophenia into a euphoric description of digital culture.

10 Compare discussions of increasing connectivity in organization theory (Kolb et al. 2012).

11 For a representative critique, see Feifer 2013.

12 For a feminist critique of the contemporary politics of withdrawal, see Sarah Sharma's 2017 Marshall McLuhan Lecture, "Exit and the Extensions of Man," summarized in Sharma 2017.

13 For the notion of a "practice-bound imaginary," see Hyysalo 2006.

14 For Anderson, the printing press played a central role in constituting a national community.

15 See Luhmann's (1984, 62) concept of connectivity (*Anschlussfähigkeit*); for a strong reading of disconnectivity in the sense of *Anschlussunfähigkeit,* see Bjerg (2006) and Stäheli (2020).

16 On this topic, see the interview with Nicole Scheller in this volume.

17 For an overview of artistic projects with Faraday cages, see the "Feel Sound" blog: https://feelsoundproject-blog.tumblr.com. As early as 1973, the Canadian artist Tom Sherman created an aluminum Faraday cage, which provided a shield against any exterior radiation; of particular note are Catherine Richard's "Curiosity Cabinet at the End of the Millennium" (1995) as well as Jan Sterbak's "Oasis" (2000) and "Faradayyart" (2001).

18 From a prime example, see Hito Steyerl, "HOW NOT TO BE SEEN. A Fucking Didactic Educational .MOV file." (Installation) (2013).

19 On the connection between biopolitics and connectivity, see Karppi 2018, 1462 (Kindle Position).

20 For a critical take, see Hesselberth 2018b.

References

Anderson, Benedict. 2006. *Imagined Communities: Reflections on the Origin and Spread of Nationalism.* London: Verso.

Bay, Morton. 2011. *Homo Conexus: The Connected Humans.* Self-published.

Berry, David M., and Alexander R. Galloway. 2016. "A Network Is a Network Is a Network: Reflections on the Computational and the Societies of Control." *Theory, Culture & Society* 33, no. 4: 151–72.

Bjerg, Ole. 2006. "Accelerating Luhmann: Towards a Systems Theory of Ambivalence." *Theory, Culture & Society* 23, no. 5: 49–68.

Bollmer, Grant. 2016. *Inhuman Networks: Social Media and the Archaeology of Connection.* New York: Bloomsbury Academic.

Boltanski, Luc, and Ève Chiapello. 2007 [1999]. *The New Spirit of Capitalism,* trans. Gregory Elliott. New York: Verso.

boyd, danah. 2004. "Love to Apophenia." *Apophenia,* February 27. Accessed April 12, 2020. http://www.zephoria.org/thoughts/archives/2004/02/27/love_to_apophenia.html.

Chun, Wendy Hui Kyong. 2006. *Control and Freedom: Power and Paranoia in the Age of Fiber Optics.* Cambridge, UK: MIT Press.

Cain, Susan. 2013. *Quiet: The Power of Introverts in a World That Can't Stop Talking.* New York: Crown.

Conrad, Klaus. 1958. *Die beginnende Schizophrenie: Versuch einer Gestaltanalyse des Wahns.* Stuttgart: Thieme.

de Certeau, Michel. 1984. *The Practice of Everyday Life,* trans. Steven Rendall. Berkeley: University of California Press.

Digital Detox®. 2020. "Camp Grounded: Summer Camp for Adults." *Digital Detox.* Accessed April 12, 2020. https://www.digitaldetox.com/experiences/camp-grounded.

Duga, Ludovic. 1922. *Les Grands Timides.* Paris: Alcan.

"Feel Sound" blog. Accessed April 28, 2020. https://feelsoundproject-blog.tumblr.com.

Feifer, Jason. 2013. "Offices for All! Why Open-Office Layouts Are Bad for Employees, Bosses, and Productivity." *Fastcompany,* November 4. Accessed April 12, 2020.

https://www.fastcompany.com/3019758/offices-for-all-why-open-office-layouts-are-bad-for-employees-bosses-and-productivity/.

Galloway, Alexander R., and Jason R. LaRiviere. 2017. "Compression in Philosophy." *boundary 2: An International Journal of Literature and Culture* 44, no. 1: 125–47.

Gaycken, Sandro, and Michael Karger. 2011. "Entnetzung statt Vernetzung: Paradigmenwechsel bei der IT-Sicherheit." *Multimedia und Recht* 3:3–8.

Hesselberth, Pepita. 2018a. "Connect, Disconnect, Reconnect: Historicizing the Current Gesture towards Disconnectivity, from the Plug-in Drug to the Digital Detox." *Cinéma&Cie: International Film Studies Journal* 30 (XVII): 105–14.

Hesselberth, Pepita. 2018b. "Discourses on Disconnectivity and the Right to Disconnect." *New Media & Society* 20, no. 5: 1994–2010.

Hyysalo, Sampsa. 2006. "Representations of Use and Practice-Bound Imaginaries in Automating the Safety of the Elderly." *Social Studies of Science* 36, no. 4: 599–626.

Jackson, Michael, and Albert Piette, eds. 2015. *What Is Existential Anthropology?* New York: Berghahn Books.

Jasanoff, Sheila. 2015. "Future Imperfect: Science, Technology, and the Imaginations of Modernity." In *Dreamscapes of Modernity: Sociotechnical Imaginaries and the Fabrication of Power,* ed. Sheila Jasanoff and Sang-Hyun Kim, 1–33. Chicago: University of Chicago Press.

Jauréguiberry, Francis. 2014. "La Déconnexion aux Technologies de Communication." *Réseaux* 186, no. 4: 15–49.

Jurgenson, Nathan. 2013. "The Disconnectionists." *The New Inquiry,* November 13. Accessed April 12, 2020. https://thenewinquiry.com/the-disconnectionists/.

Karppi, Tero. 2018. *Disconnect: Facebook's Affective Bonds.* Minneapolis: University of Minnesota Press.

Kolb, Darl G., Arran Caza, and Paul D. Collins. 2012. "States of Connectivity: New Questions and New Directions." *Organization Studies* 33, no. 2: 267–73.

Kulwin, Noah. 2018. "'There's a Little Bit of Well, We're All Just at Harvard, So What Could Happen?': A Conversation with Former Zuckerberg Speechwriter Kate Losse on How the Facebook Founder Thinks and What Is Hardest for Him to Wrap His Mind Around." *New York Magazine* 4. Accessed March 3, 2020. http://nymag.com/intelligencer/2018/04/kate-losse-former-zuckerberg-speechwriter-interview.html.

Langenohl, Andreas. 2019. "The Imaginary of the Democratic Vote: A Conceptual Contribution to Cultural Political Sociology." *Österreichische Zeitschrift für Soziologie* 44, no. 2: 57–75.

Latour, Bruno. 2002. "Gabriel Tarde and the End of the Social." In *The Social in Question: New Bearings in History and the Social Sciences,* ed. Patrick Joyce, 117–32. London: Routledge.

Latour, Bruno. 2005. *Reassembling the Social: An Introduction to Actor-Network-Theory.* New York: Oxford University Press.

Levine, Carolyn. 2015. *Forms: Whole, Rhythm, Hierarchy, Network.* Princeton, N.J.: Princeton University Press, 2015.

Llamas, Rosa, and Russell Belk. 2013. "Living in a Digital World." In *The Routledge Companion to Digital Consumption,* ed. Russell W. Belk and Rosa Llamas, 1–13. New York: Routledge.

Luhmann, Niklas. 1984. *Soziale Systeme: Grundriss einer allgemeinen Theorie.* Frankfurt am Main: Suhrkamp.

Mannell, Kate. 2017. "Technology, Resistance, and de Certeau: Deceptive Texting as a Tactic of Everyday Life." *PLATFORM: Journal of Media & Communication* 8, no. 1: 40–55.

McCullough, Malcolm. 2013. *Ambient Commons: Attention in the Age of Embodied Information.* Cambridge, Mass.: MIT Press.

Mckinlay, Alan, Chris Carter, Eric Pezet, and Stewart Clegg. 2009. "Using Foucault to Make Strategy." *Accounting, Auditing & Accountability Journal* 23, no. 8: 1012–31.

Papacharissi, Zizi. 2002. "The Virtual Sphere: The Internet as a Public Sphere." *New Media & Society* 4, no. 1: 9–27.

Pedersen, Morten A. 2013. "The Fetish of Connectivity." In *Objects and Materials: A Routledge Companion,* ed. Penny Harvey et al., 197–207. London: Routledge.

Pine, B. Joseph, and James H. Gilmore. 2011. *The Experience Economy.* Boston, Mass.: Harvard Business Press.

Portwood-Stacer, Laura. 2013. "Media Refusal and Conspicuous Non-Consumption: The Performative and Political Dimensions of Facebook Abstention." *New Media & Society* 15, no. 7: 1041–57.

Shamir, Ronen. 2008. "The Age of Responsibilization: On Market-Embedded Morality." *Economy and Society* 37, no. 1: 1–19. https://doi.org/10.1080/03085140701760833.

Sharma, Sarah. 2017. "Exit and the Extensions of Man." *transmediale Journal,* May 8. Accessed April 28, 2020. https://transmediale.de/content/exit-and-the-extensions-of-man.

Shirky, Clay. 2011. "The Political Power of Social Media: Technology, The Public Sphere, and Political Change." *Foreign Affairs* 90, no. 1: 28–41.

Simmel, Georg. 1950. "The Metropolis and Mental Life." In *The Sociology of Georg Simmel,* trans. and ed. Kurt H. Wolff, 409–24. New York: Free Press.

Simmel, Georg. 2009. *Sociology: Inquiries into the Construction of Social Forms,* vol. 2. Trans. Anthony J. Blasi, Anton K. Jacobs, and Mathew Kanjirathinkal. Boston, Mass.: Brill, 2009.

Sprenger, Florian. 2019. "Kann man das Internet abschalten?" *POP-ZEITSCHRIFT,* March 11. Accessed April 28, 2020. https://pop-zeitschrift.de/2019/03/11/kann-man-das-internet-abschalten-von-florian-sprenger11-3-2019/.

Stäheli, Urs. 2013. "Die Angst vor der Gemeinschaft." *Merkur* 67 (773): 928–40.

Stäheli, Urs. 2018. "Distanz und Indifferenz." In *Georg Simmel und das Leben in der Gegenwart,* ed. Rüdiger Lautmann and Hans Wienold, 169–91. Wiesbaden: Springer VS.

Stäheli, Urs. 2020. *Soziologie der Entnetzung.* Frankfurt am Main: Suhrkamp.

Stäheli, Urs, and Luise Stoltenberg. 2020. "Digital Detox Tourism: Practices of Analogization" (unpublished manuscript).

Steyerl, Hito. 2013. "HOW NOT TO BE SEEN. A Fucking Didactic Educational .MOV file." (Installation).

Strathern, Marilyn. 1996. "Cutting the Network." *Journal of the Royal Anthropological Institute* 2, no. 3: 517–35.

Sutton, Theodora. 2017. "Disconnect to Reconnect: The Food/Technology Metaphor in Digital Detoxing." *First Monday* 22, no. 6. doi: http://dx.doi.org/10.5210/fm.v22i16.7561.

Tarde, Gabriel. 1903 [1890]. *The Laws of Imitation.* Trans. Elsie Clews Parsons. New York: Holt.

Tonkiss, Fran. 2003. "The Ethics of Indifference: Community and Solitude in the City." *International Journal of Cultural Studies* 6, no. 3: 297–311.

van Dijck, José. 2013. *The Culture of Connectivity: A Critical History of Social Media.* Oxford: Oxford University Press.

Wigley, Mark. 2001. "Network Fever." *Grey Room* 4:82–122.

Willkens, Andre. 2015. *Analog ist das neue Bio: Navigationshilfe durch unsere digitale Welt.* Berlin: Metrolit.

Wortham, Jenna. 2009. "The Value of a Facebook Friend? About 37 Cents." *The New York Times,* January 9.

Zehle, Soenke. 2014. "Reclaiming the Ambient Commons: Strategies of Depletion Design in the Subjective Economy." *International Review of Information Ethics* 22:31–42.

ZEIT Online. 2020. "Grüne wollen Recht auf Mobilfunk festschreiben." *Die Zeit,* January 13. Accessed April 28, 2020. https://www.zeit.de/politik/deutschland/2020-01/netzausbau-funkloecher-mobilfunk-gruene.

Zuboff, Shoshana. 2019. *The Age of Surveillance Capitalism: The Fight for a Human Future at the New Frontier of Power.* New York: PublicAffairs.

Zuckerberg, Randi. 2013. *Dot Complicated: Untangling Our Wired Lives.* New York: Harper Collins.

[2]

Confusing Algorithms and Undoing Body Shapes: An Interview with Fashion Designer Nicole Scheller

Lea P. Zierott
Translated by Erik Born

Fashion designer Nicole Scheller studied applied arts in Schneeberg, Germany. She graduated in 2017 with her IP/privacy collection, which presented antisurveillance fashion. Since then, her work has focused on the question of how to make fashion an instrument for protecting the private sphere against digital surveillance, especially by using special materials. Scheller lives and works in Leipzig, Germany, where the following interview was conducted in January 2020.

LEA P. ZIEROTT: How can clothing make someone disappear?

NICOLE SCHELLER: Well, I decided to work with clothing in the first place because I'm a fashion designer. But when it comes down to it, surveillance cameras are really concerned with people's identities. Algorithms, too, biometrics, are really about identity. Biometrics are essentially *patterns* that translate someone's identity into a simple mathematical form for an algorithm. On the basis of someone's biometrics, an algorithm knows that they are X or Y, and now it knows what they look like. Fashion works exactly the same in some respects. We wear fashion or clothing to express ourselves, to transport our identities to the outside world. But fashion can also protect people from the outside world. It's so effective because people can play a lot with shapes and forms. Large shapes, for instance, can conceal one's gender. Size, weight—people can easily play with these categories by concealing their identifying features. Clothing is such a simple and effective way of protecting oneself against all this biometric data collection. It's really the simplest path anyone could take.

As for the patterns, which are still in the development phase, they confuse algorithms even more about the surfaces of things. By producing meaningless data, people can make it even more difficult for algorithms to identify anyone at all. The first step is really about identification and only the second one is about analysis. Even in the first step, someone can already succeed in convincing an algorithm that they don't count as a person—for instance, by totally scattering their external form. That's a pretty good way of protecting oneself against surveillance, especially because most algorithms used for the initial recognition process operate in real time, which means they have to evaluate an enormous amount of data in a very short amount of time. That's why the recognition process is very prone to errors and people can still react in time. Still, it's always tilting at windmills. I only need to take a look at new developments and locate the sources of error and then I can go and try to find new solutions.

LZ: So, people are still identified but as something else?

NS: Anyone can make identification more difficult, so to speak. There's a university in China, I think, that has developed another pattern like this one, which makes algorithms fail to recognize that the objects they're observing are human beings.[1] That would be the next step to take. I'm definitely not there yet. Everything is still in the test phase. Unfortunately, things aren't so far along that someone could walk right past a surveillance camera and not be identified at all. But anyone can make identification more difficult, and that's good enough for now. You'll either be falsely identified or you'll produce meaningless data, which means even more data, which the algorithm might not be able to compute. The kind of data that doesn't make any sense for identification, like a person with ten faces. It doesn't make sense. It might fall through the cracks. But it falsifies the entire data set by producing meaningless information about external forms. Reflecting also plays a role in some surveillance systems, especially if they're made up of 3D scanners, which is already quite common. They work with infrared light that people can easily confuse with reflectors. Those are some of the strategies I've found in my work so far, but I'm still working on them. We'll see what happens next.

LZ: How does the process of disappearing, or not being able to be identified, work? Is it a simple "yes-or-no"—you put something on and then you're no longer identifiable? Or are there intermediate steps?

NS: As I was saying, anyone can always still be recognized as a human being. But I try to interfere with the process of identification, so that someone can really only be recognized as a human being and not as a particular person. That's one kind of intermediate step. Of course, I'm playing with biometrics and body shapes to make things *really strange.* This kind of estrangement is the focus of my collection.

LZ: You named your label IP/privacy. Can you tell us how it came about and how you came up with the idea of making this form of fashion in the first place?

NS: I didn't want to simply take up the topic of surveillance and exclusively produce fashion. That's not a challenge for me, personally. I like to find various ways of solving a problem. Whenever I identify a problem, I want to offer at least one potential solution, and that worked extremely well for this particular project and this particular subject. Of course, then I came across Adam Harvey and took a look at what was going on in that direction.[2] At the time, there were already a couple of other artists. That was back in 2014, when everything started popping up out of the ground with the whole NSA scandal. When I was getting started with my own work around three years later, I noticed that everything had gotten stuck. Things weren't getting better. They were getting worse. And I thought, "Why aren't you doing something about it anymore?"

LZ: Your "way of solving a problem," I mean your *collection*—What parts does it consist of and how do they work?

NS: The collection can be divided into two main categories. I approached everything from the bottom up. So first I looked at what kinds of surveillance systems there are, which ones are already being used, what can be found in urban spaces, and I started coming across infrared cameras, more in private usage. And then there were the automated face-recognition trials at the Südkreuz train station in Berlin, which are supposed to be expanded throughout the entire country. So, I looked at how they function. How does an algorithm identify someone's face? What role do biometrics play? How does the recognition process work? What possibilities are there for face recognition and motion analysis?

At first, I concentrated on face recognition and dealt a little with motion analysis. That resulted in the black-and-white knits—the three oversized pieces in the collection with an asymmetrical, black-and-white pattern. I deliberately used asymmetry and the large size to conceal the shape of the body. It was the simplest way of doing it. The long and voluminous shapes cover up all the nodal points needed for motion analysis—knees, hips, arms—and that makes it more difficult. It's not 100 percent perfect, it's a way of creating some "obstacles" for motion analysis. Another thing that spurred me on was to avoid creating burkas, which would completely enclose the wearer.[3] It was important for me to keep the face open and to make clothes that people could wear on the street. Of course, the pieces look very different when you first see them, but they work as streetwear. They're wearable. They'll

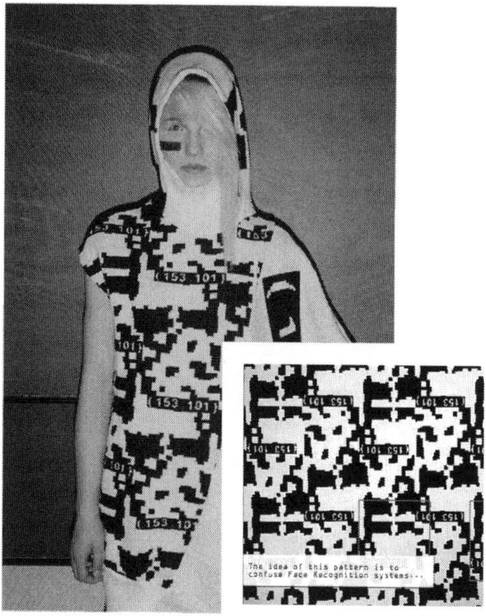

[Figure 2.1]. Nicole Scheller, *IP/privacy,* 2017, black and white pattern. Photograph by Franz Grünewald; Christina Dalbert, model.

definitely attract attraction but not from the cameras, and that's the point.

The black-and-white pattern came out of my attempts to incorporate biometrics and analyze how they function. How does an algorithm recognize our faces, and what does the network it works with look like? I played around with it a little and developed this pattern. When an algorithm scans the pattern, it'll recognize something, which I then used to create duplicate faces. Thanks to the large number of faces and their positions, which together make up the black-and-white face pattern, the algorithm can no longer clearly say that this particular person is X or Y.

One piece in my collection is an oversized bomber jacket, which is intended to cover up the nodal points needed for motion analysis entirely. It goes down to the knees

[Figure 2.2]. Nicole Scheller, *IP/privacy*, 2017, bomber jacket. Photograph by Franz Grünewald; Christina Dalbert, model.

and makes whoever's wearing it look like a great big egg. There's also a slight hump in the back, which defragments the entire shape of the body. I didn't use a pattern for any of it. I wanted to get back to the general idea of destroying the shape of the body and the question of how we can respond to motion analysis.

LZ: And the main point of this material is that it takes on a shape of its own?

NS: That it holds its own shape as much as possible. I'm bad at using silk, it always collapses on me, which is why I'm always on the search for fabrics that retain their shape. That's also behind my choice of contrasting colors, which was hardly random. The algorithm looks for extreme contrasts, which is why a black-and-white pattern is good at preventing someone from being recognized. I ended up sticking with these two colors, black and white.

There's another oversized bomber jacket, which I also used for the cut of the white jacket (see Figure 2.2). It's made out of a different fabric but it's still a knit that holds its shape well, and there's another nice hump in the back, which also holds its shape relatively well. And here, of course, there's another oversized sweater.

I also designed a dress where the pattern worked pretty well. I took a video with it hanging on the dress form, which shows how the algorithm tries to recognize faces even in the straps.

LZ: So if someone wears this dress and steps in front of a surveillance camera, it wouldn't only see one face, it'd see ten faces?

NS: Exactly, that was the idea, at least. That's why it was important for me to keep the face visible but at the same time to produce meaningless data that would make any clear identification more difficult. Somehow, seeing a person with ten faces doesn't make sense to the algorithm.

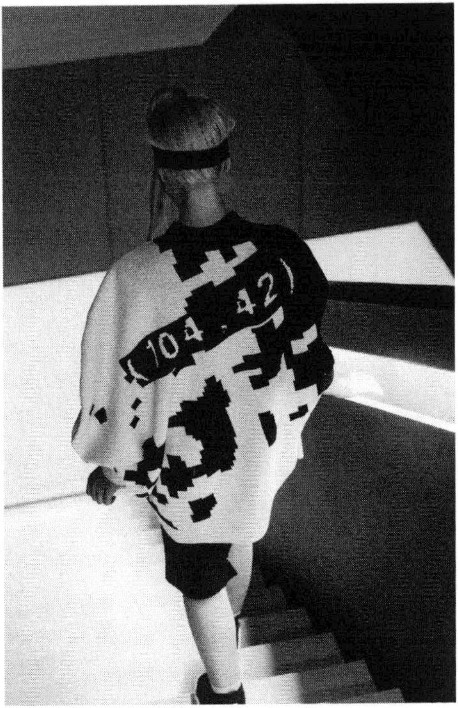

[Figure 2.3]. Nicole Scheller, *IP/privacy,* 2017, sweater. Photograph by Franz Grünewald; Christina Dalbert, model.

There must be an error and everything would theoretically need to be analyzed again, but by that point you're already long gone. So, the point is to produce errors as quickly and effectively as possible, in real time—right in the real-time scan, as it were—so that you won't be recognized. It worked really well with this pattern, I even tested it out with different sizes. In some cases, the pattern ends up getting divided into even smaller sections, which creates even more faces.

LZ: It really is a stylish pattern. At least, I don't think it'd be that weird to wear it. It's a little like houndstooth, don't you think?

NS: Yes, definitely. That would be one face the camera would recognize. Add to that your own face and then there would be two faces, which confuses the algorithm. The numbers in the pattern were originally part of the programming process. But I only kept them in for aesthetic reasons. Because they were related to programming, I thought, "Come on, just leave it in! Someone will think that something is off here; it must mean something!"

That was the one piece. The other one was actually just a coat where I integrated LEDs into the hood to create a sort of "fade effect" for infrared or night-vision cameras. Now, the way the effect works isn't exactly that someone can just walk down the street and literally light up like a lightbulb. The fade occurs beyond our visual spectrum and can only be seen by the camera. The piece also has a special IRR coating, which is normally used in the military. It's especially confusing for thermal-imaging cameras,

[Figure 2.4]. Nicole Scheller, *IP/privacy,* 2017, coat. Photograph by Franz Grünewald; Christina Dalbert, model.

since it keeps all of your body heat inside. You're practically invisible, or only visible as a smudge in the image. It's used less in urban spaces. But it was still a great fit because I was dealing with infrared. You switch on the LEDs in the hood before you get going.

LZ: And they light up all around your head?

NS: Precisely. The hood itself is very large, as is the neckline. You can't recognize anyone's face, no matter what perspective you look at it from. I tested it out with video recordings, and it works great from the front and the side. Nobody can see anything, since the wearer is completely illuminated.

The angle of the LEDs and the wavelength of light are designed in a way that they completely blind the infrared camera. An infrared camera needs light to see in the dark, and the LEDs simply send this light right back to it. That's what created the idea of reflecting, as well as this bright glow. Once again, it's in the coating. It's a really tough material, which doesn't let any body heat pass through to the outside, and that ensures that people aren't seen by drones. Unfortunately, I haven't had the chance to test it out with a thermal camera yet, though I'd love to see the results.

LZ: But wouldn't you also have to make sure that no body heat escapes through the zipper or the seams?

NS: Theoretically, I would have had to make a whole suit. In my coat, you can see the wearer's hands, because it was designed for an urban space. Otherwise, you'd sweat like a pig in it, since the material is so tough. That's why I made it as large as possible, so that even the sleeves are a little more open. Otherwise, you'd really sweat like a dog. Those are the kinds of things you only ever notice during the initial development. I did everything in half a year, including the technical development, the materials, and the cuts. Nothing else was possible for the time being. Of course, these are the kinds of things you need to keep on your radar for future development, or else it won't work. Nobody will wear it.

Then there are the basics, which I sewed for people to wear under the collection, to preserve the asymmetry. There are bumps here too. I also designed a kind of visor that you can wear like a cap. It doesn't let in any infrared light, and your face looks like a dark disk—you're unrecognizable. Then there are leggings with "chub-knees"—that's what I like to call them because they make your knees look chubby but in a good way. Of course, I'm often just playing around. But I'm serious about asymmetry and the potential defragmentation of the human body, ideas that inform my entire collection.

Figure 2.5. Nicole Scheller, *IP/privacy,* 2017, visor. Photograph by Franz Grünewald; Christina Dalbert, model.

After the collection, I also started a small line of antisurveillance products like this bag. You can stick your cell phone and credit cards inside and be completely offline. I called the line of products "[*off 'lain*]." They're bonus gadgets for the collection, little things to let people decide for themselves when to be offline.

What makes it work is a particular material made of metal threads that gets incorporated into the lining. It's like you're putting your cellphone inside a lead box or an aluminum refrigerator. You're offline. Theoretically, you could just put your phone in the fridge, that works too.

LZ: The bag is really stylish though . . .

NS: It has to be—otherwise, nobody would want it. That's exactly my approach. I noticed that words like "information privacy" and "the private sphere" sounded dusty and seemed like they're none of anybody's business. That's why people can respond to surveillance so well with fashion, or at least I'm trying to. By making these words carry more weight, I'm trying to create a new discourse. What I'm trying to say is, "It's cool again, we can talk about it, everyone can do something about it, everyone can spread the message and look good doing it."

LZ: What about the hat? Is it also for antisurveillance purposes?

NS: It's a special hat, still a prototype like everything else. It'll also involve the visor concept, but I'm still working on the mechanics. These are all new ideas of things to come. The main point is to protect people's identities. When it comes to evading surveillance, nobody has a real choice. If someone puts up a surveillance camera, there's really nothing anybody else can do about it. You can respond with your choice of clothing, maybe put on a hoodie or something. But in the end, there's not much else you can do to protect your identity. You're going to be filmed somewhere and you can't protect yourself against it. When it comes to biometrics, we're an open book. It's all really shady. If you're being evaluated all the time, like with the rewards and punishments in China's social credit system, and you happen to run a red light with a traffic camera, then wham—minus ten points! Today, it's no longer Orwell, it's the real world.

LZ: Would you describe your fashion as unisex, or does it matter who wears it?

NS: Theoretically, it's all tailored in a particular way. The cuts are all very wide, or they don't really have anything to do with a normal cut. But for menswear, I'd have to make everything a little larger, because people are built differently. My larger ambition is to make two lines, or maybe just one line, but it's definitely gender-neutral. Anyone can wear it. In terms of customer demand, those looking for menswear tend to prefer the coat, those looking for womenswear the black-and-white pattern. But different people think different things are cool. I get the craziest requests.

LZ: And now you're getting a lot of requests, since people can see photos of the clothes on your website?

NS: That's for sure. I recently got a request from one guy who thought the black-and-white pattern was really cool and wanted to have it on a suit blazer. It's a good idea, but I'm not that far along yet.

LZ: Does that mean you're still in development, or are your clothes already being worn on the street?

NS: Well, I've been tinkering around for most of the past year with making the cellphone bag into a product. I even sold a couple of prototypes. But everything is still in the development phase, even the clothes. And I definitely won't get very far working on my own. I lack the technical know-how to be able to say, "Now, I'm going to do something with automated face recognition." I depend on other people to help me out. It would be nice to have a team with a computer programmer and someone who does business management and keep working from there. That's why it took me a while to get everything up and running to the point where it could really take off.

One of my goals is to make sure that the entire collection can function as streetwear in everyday situations. If the collection gets put in an exhibition or a museum, it'll just sit there, and it won't help anyone. Sure, it might stimulate the discourse. But I really want to help people help themselves. Like I said, everyone should be able to make their own decisions and do something for themselves, for the private sphere, because that's precisely what's being subject to more and more restrictions. It was important for me to really *get to the bottom* of this point.

LZ: Would the computer programmer in your hypothetical team be the one responsible for making sure that the algorithms work, then?

NS: Sure. By now, I have a basic understanding of algorithms, I really have to. But I definitely can't get that deep into the material, so the programmer could do that work for me. Of course, they would also have to see what's possible. They couldn't do everything on their own either. We'd probably need a whole technical team to disassemble the algorithms. To pull off anything truly great, I'm dependent on others. I'd be happy to have a team.

LZ: But your main task would be translating everything into the material or the clothing?

NS: Sure. There would need to be at least three different areas of development, and I would need to "translate," as you put it, so that everything *works* and can be implemented. We'll see.

LZ: When you say that it takes a year to make something

like the bag, what does this process look like? What exactly are you doing?

NS: Above all, I'm relying on my materials. It's not the case that I can simply pick up a silk fabric and work with it. I need to inspect my materials very closely to discover their abilities. I've done lots of tests with the metal weave, for instance, which has worked the best so far for making fasteners. It's a simple product, but it wasn't easy to make it truly shielded and in a way that's also easy for the end user. That was the crux of the whole thing, and so there's a lot of trial and error in these products.

LZ: What does one of your trials look like, then, say, with the jacket?

NS: Put it on, try it out, look at the algorithm, get it scanned. The jacket basically works but not to the point where someone could just go to the Südkreuz train station and not be recognized. It's definitely not there yet. But I've found the approach I'd like to keep pursuing. I've gotten a hell of a lot of requests from people who really want to buy the clothes. But I'm not really ready to sell them yet. Sure, someone could wear one of the pieces as a fashion statement. But for me, the real point of wearing them is to be almost invisible, and that needs to work really well. I want to take my time and think everything through, so everyone will just have to wait.

LZ: Could you describe your search for materials? How do you come up with something?

NS: Research. You can always find something in military technology. Shielding products are one small sector that's been around for ages, with offices, for instance, where sensitive data or electronic parts get stored in certain rooms. So, you can look and see where something like that already exists, and then instead of just thinking that it's strange, you can use it in a strange way. Something always ends up working a little. It's research, pure and simple. Identifying the problem and the appropriate materials, and then looking around and testing things out. I like to order various materials, try them out, and see whether or not they work.

LZ: And then the material needs to be workable . . .

NS: Exactly, like with the coat. It's a Cordura fabric with IRR coating, a really strong material. Today, I would never even work with it, because it's too stiff, like backpack material, and it's not comfortable for everyday use. At one point in time, it was a good solution, but it no longer works for the end user. Those are the kinds of things I have in mind for the next developments, what could work better. How do people make things with LEDs, for instance? It's a completely new field for me, which LEDs to use, whether they're washable, these kinds of things. They're very important, especially if you want to sell a piece. It's all still just one big experiment that's only starting to get exciting.

LZ: You also work with this particular shade of black . . .

NS: Vantablack. I came across it at one point or another; it was another research project. It's practically the *blackest black* there is.[4] Because it absorbs light completely, so to speak. It's a carbon color, which means that you can think of it like a forest—any light that falls on the forest will get swallowed up.[5] It's really dark there, and the structure of the color is similar. I found it really exciting, but the main problem is that it's not really durable. It doesn't last for very long after you apply it, and you can't just apply it anywhere, since it can be wiped off afterwards. That's why it's not yet practical for me. I'm excited to see what kinds of developments there will be as the years go by. I don't have time for it at the moment, it's another completely different field that has taken years to get to this point. The possibility of using it for something else, like a varnish or a deliberately washable paint, now that would be super exciting, and I'd definitely have a few pieces ready to go.

LZ: What kinds of things has Vantablack been used for up to now?

NS: Good question. I don't know whether it was developed by NASA or someone else. The only thing I know is that there's a company that copied it, because up to now anyone who wanted to use this blackest black needed a license for it.

Of course, the license costs a hell of a lot of money, which created a countermovement of people saying, "We want to use this shade of black and we're going to do our own research." They actually even developed a color and brought it to market. It's intended more for artists and painters and other creative types. But even this new shade of black is still washable. So, it's not really durable and not really useful for me yet. But I'd love to make something with it, if only it would last a little longer, that would be really cool. Like I said, let's wait and see what happens.

Again, I'm very reliant on my materials. I can't just say, "I've got an idea, I'd like to implement it now." These are fields where people have been doing research for years! That's why I have to see what's available on the market and how I can use it for my own purposes.

LZ: How did you manage to get the anti-face recognition pattern with all the faces on it into the fabric?

NS: That's the cool thing about biometrics—you can do a lot with surface design. It doesn't really matter what kind of material you're working with. The main point is that the algorithm recognizes it. And as soon as that happens, it works. As a designer, you can indulge yourself, which I personally find to be pretty great. That my work as a designer doesn't depend on the material for once—which is often quite pleasant, don't get me wrong. But the possibility of playing with the design without thinking about the material, that's a really nice change for me.

LZ: Does surface design mean that you still make the fabrics yourself?

NS: Well, in part. Like I said, I knitted the pattern into the knit piece. I didn't dye it, I knitted directly into it. That's why it's permanently integrated and works well right from the start. The algorithm recognizes it, anyway, and that's a pretty good first step.

LZ: Do you have the sense that antisurveillance clothing, or clothing for disconnection, is a topic in the fashion world right now?

NS: Phew! It's not, not at all. Well, at most with these RFID-blocking products. I think there was a Hugo Boss suit at some point with a little breast pocket with an RFID-blocker inside it, for credit cards and stuff like that. That was the only thing people were going on about for a little while. In the past few years, I've seen lots of RFID blocking wallets. But the problem is that most of them are made with bad materials. They only last two weeks and then they fall apart. Or, you end up washing them, and then they're toast. The people who make these things aren't thinking about whether they'll really work in the long term.

As for disconnection or the private sphere, I haven't personally heard of many attempts to really address these topics, and if so, then only in small circles of artists. It takes a lot of courage to deal with these things, and they're still hot topics for big labels and large companies. They're politically loaded, and the businesses usually aren't up for it. They stick to the motto: "Keep everything as neat as possible. Just do fashion, and that's enough." Well, it's not enough for me.

LZ: Apart from clothing you're also working with body

painting. Do you have a holistic notion of disconnection in your work?

NS: My main concern is clothing. Adam Harvey did something similar with painting,[6] so it was really just a little nod to his work because it went well with fashion. At the end of the day, I'm spending most of my time on biometrics, which naturally includes the face. It's a massive undertaking to deal with the whole pattern, but my own work ultimately keeps going in the direction of fashion. My clothes are already extreme. It would be too much for someone to wear something else on their face, like makeup. Nobody would do it. Well, nobody would do it *seriously.* Maybe at a rave or something, but not in everyday life.

LZ: Would you say then that your main design concept is about making sure that the clothes are wearable?

NS: Definitely. You could even say, "form follows function," because I have to get my bearings from two extreme directions, from the end user, the wearer, and from the [surveillance] systems. Everything needs to be based on how the cameras work, how they see someone, and I have to adapt my design in that direction. That's why I'm always trying to find out what the problem really is and how we might respond to it. That's the entire content of my work. Really, I'm a problem solver, at least I'm always looking for potential solutions.

LZ: Let me conclude then by thanking you very much for this interesting conversation.

Notes

1 For further details on the "invisibility cloak" project, which actually resulted from a collaboration between Tsinghua University and the University of Washington, see Yang et al. 2018.

2 In 2013, Berlin-based artist and researcher Adam Harvey brought out his Stealth Wear collection, which consisted of antidrone fashion. Harvey's CV

Dazzle collection also deals with antisurveillance products and camouflage techniques. See Harvey's website, https://ahprojects.com/.

3 Scheller appears to be contrasting her work again with Harvey's Stealth Wear collection, which was "inspired by traditional Islamic dress and the idea that garments can provide a separation between *man* and God" (Harvey 2012).

4 On Vantablack, which was developed by Surrey NanoSystems, see the company's website, https://www.surreynanosystems.com/about/vantablack. On the reception of one artist's attempt to patent the color, see "Black 3.0: Anish Kapoor and the Art World's Pettiest, Funniest Dispute," *The Guardian*, August 5, 2019.

5 See the entry for "Forest" in the Glossary of this volume.

6 In his CV Dazzle collection, Harvey uses a facial camouflage technique inspired by the naval camouflage developed during the First World War and colloquially known as "razzle dazzle"; see the revised 2020 version of Harvey's collection, updated a decade after the original collection, https://cvdazzle.com/.

References

"Black 3.0: Anish Kapoor and the Art World's Pettiest, Funniest Dispute." 2019. *The Guardian*, August 5. Accessed April 22, 2020. https://www.theguardian.com/artanddesign/shortcuts/2019/aug/05/black-30-anish-kapoor-and-the-art-worlds-pettiest-funniest-dispute.

Harvey, Adam R. 2012. "Stealth Wear." *AH Projects*, March 12. Accessed April 22, 2020. https://ahprojects.com/stealth-wear/.

Yang, Darren Y., et al. 2018. "Building Towards 'Invisible Cloak': Robust Physical Adversarial Attack on YOLO Object Detector." *9th IEEE Annual Ubiquitous Computing, Electronics & Mobile Communication Conference (UEMCON)*, 368–74. New York, N.Y. Accessed April 22, 2020. doi: 10.1109/UEMCON.2018.8796670.

[3]

Undoing the Outside: On Defaults and Off-Facebook Activity

Tero Karppi

> I was recently online on my computer when I noticed that the ads on the sides of the screen were for Ashley Madison. I do not think my husband is cheating, I really don't, but I still get that jealous pang in my chest when this happens. Is it possible that those ads are showing up because of websites I visit? . . . So, am I just in denial? Or is it possible these ads are my fault, and if so, is there a way to stop them from showing up?

When a concerned Internet user posed these questions to *Slate's* sex advice column, columnist Rich Juzwiak (2019) emphasized the irony of turning the site into a "very basic tech advice column." Underscoring his lack of technical experience, Juzwiak came immediately to a larger conclusion: "It is true that sometimes previous visits to a website could result in targeted ads for that site, but that's not the only thing generating such content," Juzwiak answers. Targeting potential customers, he continues, "is a fuzzy science, and major screw-ups have occurred in this very realm. It was recently reported that ads for Ashley Madison appeared on multiple children's sites." Juzwiak's answer indicates that ads for a dating site once marketed primarily to users looking for extramarital affairs are not necessarily connected to having a profile on Ashley Madison or even visiting that particular website. Rather, the ads result from more abstract demographic targeting of potential customers. For anyone familiar with how targeted advertising works in the social media age, this method is nothing new. Users are constantly placed in cookie-cutter audiences based on their age, location, and occupation; visitors are bombarded with tailored ads based on not only the websites they frequent but also those of their presumed peers. What is new, as Juzwiak's response notes, is that major social platforms such as Twitter and Facebook have begun to offer users the ability to "opt-out" of personalized targeted marketing. In other words, users can now block the flow of information among Ashley Madison, Facebook, Google, and similar sites, thereby reducing the chances of receiving unwanted ads and perhaps calming those with suspicious minds. These opt-out capabilities are not designed exclusively for those with something to hide but for everyone who wants to have more control over the ads they see when they use social platforms.

In this chapter, I will focus specifically on Facebook's Off-Facebook Activity tool (Facebook A). This tool, which the company rolled out on August 20, 2019, can be contextualized as Facebook's solution to the aforementioned problem of social media connectivity brought about by personalized targeted advertising. When users are connected to Facebook's highly intensive algorithmic structure, the data generated from their heterogenous online activities become the means for identifying, profiling, and targeting them regardless of their wishes. In the past few years, this problem has received increased media attention, exemplified by the high-profile case of Cambridge Analytica and its psychographic profiling and targeting of voters based on Facebook data. The possibility to disconnect some of the data streams used for targeting now becomes part of the user's "Facebook experience" (Facebook B). The tool, which one can access from one's Facebook settings, gives a "summary of your [user] activity that we [Facebook] receive from businesses or organizations, which includes your activity on other apps and websites" (Facebook C). This information is used by Facebook to "show more relevant ads"; suggest things that could interest the users such as events, Marketplace items, and groups; help the user to find new businesses and brands and help the latter to understand "how their website, app or ads are performing and whether they're reaching the right people"; and to identify "suspicious activity" (Facebook C). With the tool you can not only review a summary of your past Off-Facebook Activity but also "You can disconnect your past off-Facebook activity from your account with the clear history control in your off-Facebook activity setting," Facebook (B) tells us.

According to the prevailing logic, the perceived problem (connectivity) and its standard solution (disconnection) are seen as binary opposites. The empirical and conceptual analysis of the Off-Facebook Activity tool in this chapter is intended to argue that this relation is productive rather than disruptive. Seeing the relation between connection and disconnection as productive refers to what Pepita Hesselberth (2018) calls the "structuring paradox" of disconnection: there is no connectivity without disconnectivity. My analysis will build on Hesselberth's view of disconnection as a process that does not negate connectivity but gives rise to an outside that is immanently present (2018, 2007). The constitution of the outside is at the heart of my reading of the Off-Facebook Activity tool, which designates the outside with a specific name: "off-Facebook." I claim that this term denotes a particular mode of exteriority defined by the company and manifest in how the tool works and is contextualized. The argument I develop in this chapter is that the Off-Facebook Activity tool implies Facebook's incapability to think above and beyond the dominant images of current connectivity—the relation they have themselves effectively constructed, where connections that contribute data for the company are essential for its financial survival.

In the following, I map out how the Off-Facebook Activity tool is said to "undo" the links between the platform, its users, and advertisers. The slogan for the Off-Facebook Activity tool is "You see it. You control it," which emphasizes that while the platform offers the tools, privacy is a *user choice* (Facebook L). Focusing on the problematics of choice, and following Deepti Singh Apte's lead, I will use nudge theory to discuss the tool as a choice architecture that gives users an explicit sense of autonomy by providing them with control over their privacy settings while still subjecting them to an environment where other modes of control operate, often beyond users' awareness (Apte 2020). In my reading the control over privacy settings is privacy controlled by the company, and the definition of off-Facebook activity is an attempt to redraw the boundaries of connectivity.

My main sources for the analysis are the promotional videos, which introduces the Off-Facebook Activity tool, and which in my reading influence user behavior and direct users toward certain practices instead of others. I will analyze four videos included in the tool's promotional website (Facebook A): "Meera Introduces Our New Data Control to Her Husband" (Facebook D), "Introducing Off-Facebook Activity: A New Tool That Gives You More Control of Your Data" (Facebook L), "Why Do Ads Feel Like They Are Directed to You, Personally?" (Facebook J), and "Where Online Advertising is Headed" (Facebook K).[1] All together, the materials for close reading in this chapter consist of the platform's official promotional materials, help-center documents that describe the tool or the company's definition of off-Facebook activity, and other Facebook materials that describe how ad targeting works (Facebook A–L). As I will show, the discourses of the Off-Facebook Activity tool nudge users to evaluate their choice to disconnect in terms of gains and losses, often encouraging them to keep using the system rather than abandon it. In the end, I argue that we should pay attention to the ways in which the outside is constituted and imagined in the discourses of disconnection.

Incidentally, "Meera Introduces Our New Data Control to Her Husband" is the name of a video (Facebook D) Facebook uses to promote its opt-out tool "Off-Facebook Activity" and it features a happy couple.[2] In this video, Meera from Facebook's *Data and Privacy Team* shows her husband David the platform's new data controls. "We just released a control that gives people the ability to view a summary of their off-Facebook activity and disconnect that from their account," Meera explains to David. The couple conduct the interview at Facebook headquarters, where soft light flows through the translucent windows at the back of the scene. "What's Facebook activity?" David asks. Meera explains that it consists of information about users' interactions, including app usage and website visits. David asks further whether Facebook sends his name and phone number to websites after receiving indications of interactions. "No," Meera answers, firmly shaking her head. "We can show you ads without telling advertisers who you are." David asks for an example, and Meera illustrates how clicking and browsing on a backpack website creates a piece of data showing that a user on device X clicked on an image of a particular backpack. To illustrate this point, they discuss the process of shopping for a backpack, which is illustrated with animations of imaginary companies and simplified data flows. If any user clicks on any links on an affiliated shopping website, that device data will be relayed back to Facebook, matched to its own user database, and used to serve up a targeted ad. "Okay, and now, I can disconnect that if I want to," David says hesitantly. Meera asks for his phone, and an overlaid animation shows her accessing a scrollable off-Facebook activity list of 215 imaginary apps and websites that have shared David's activity with the company. "That's why I see all these backpack ads," the enlightened David deduces. "So, if I disconnect this, do *[sic]* I not see ads anymore?" Meera clarifies, "You'll still see the same number of ads. They're just gonna be less personalized." "That makes sense," rejoices David as Meera announces "more transparency and control updates to come."

Individuals are at the center of the promotional materials of the Off-Facebook Activity tool. "The best person to be in control of data is you," the press release for the Off-Facebook Activity tool declares (Facebook A). The tool's documents and videos claim, both implicitly and explicitly, that users are the best persons to control their data, and that the Off-Facebook Activity tool gives them the means to do so. Emphasizing user control and placing the burden of responsibility on individuals is hardly new. As Siva Vaidhyanathan points out, it has become a "standard position . . . of Silicon Valley companies that monitor our behavior and record our transactions" (Vaidhyanathan 2018, 74). Central to Facebook's idea of control is the idea that users have a choice to manage their privacy online. In its emphasis on choice, the Off-Facebook Activity tool also belongs to a longer history of privacy tools, which have been designed to give users more control over the leakiness of online connectivity (Chun 2016). Ever since the 1990s, the makers of these tools have envisioned privacy, as Nora Draper (2019, 87) notes, as "a function of personal choice optimized through tools that enable control." The Off-Facebook Activity tool belongs to a genealogy of tools that emphasize individuals' choice to protect their personal data in information systems, for example, by hiding their IP addresses and letting them surf the web in stealth mode (51–52). Draper underscores the importance of *enabling choice* as a function of situation-specific protection: a "user participating in a chat room, for example, might prefer to use a consistent pseudonymous persona. . . . That same individual, however, may prefer complete anonymity when visiting news sites or browsing for health-related information" (54).

Enabling the choice for privacy does not, however, solely solve what has been called the privacy paradox: that individuals are aware of privacy issues and yet choose to act against their best knowledge (Kokolakis 2017). Behavioral economists have claimed that how we evaluate the worth of privacy online depends on psychological biases such as a state of loss aversion (Acquisti, John, and Loewenstein 2013). Loss aversion holds that, for individuals, "losses are weighted substantially more than objectively commensurate gains" (Kahnemann, Knetsch, and Thaler 1990, 1326). Research on loss aversion has indicated that individuals tend to overvalue the things in their possession; for example, what one person is willing to pay for a good is less than what they are willing to accept when they sell it.[3] This behavior is not rational yet is constitutive to the decision-making process.

Ideas like loss aversion become important to the emergence of the field of nudge theory.[4] In their book *Nudge* (2008), Richard Thaler and Cass Sunstein claim that human behavior is not as rational as economists have proposed throughout the history of the field. The directing thought behind nudge theory is that human behavior cannot be controlled by relying on rationality in decision-making situations and thus people need to be "nudged" toward certain behaviors. Nudge theory is connected to an ideology Thaler and Sunstein define as "libertarian paternalism," which pushes people to make certain choices in given situations without coercion (Thaler and Sunstein 2003). This ideology presupposes an authority who knows what is best for individuals and groups, and promotes those behaviors through subtle nudges. The Social and Behavioral Science team of the Obama administration was probably the most famous example of the practical applications of this theory. Moreover, "Nudge-style forms of governance have been employed most commonly in North America and Western Europe to address lifestyle issues linked to diet, exercise and smoking, financial practices related to saving and investment, and 'anti-social' behavior such as loitering and speeding," Carolyn Pedwell observes (2017, 60). The aims of nudges are often to break bad habits, promote healthier lifestyles, and generally improve people's lives (Thaler and Sunstein 2008; Pedwell 2017; Mannevuo 2019).

One specific area of social media to which nudge theory has already been applied is the aforementioned context of privacy (Wang et al. 2014, 2367). Alessandro Acquisti (2009), for example, asserts that systems can be designed to "enhance and influence" users' privacy choices. By exposing and exploiting psychological and emotional biases users are nudged towards more informed decisions. While in this context nudging can be justified with the importance of more informed choices that protect privacy, it is clear that this technique can be applied to other purposes as well. To exemplify nudges, Thaler and Sunstein mention the practices of "collaborative filtering," which is used to provide recommendations for books, films, and other products on the basis of an individual's tastes and preferences, as well as their degree of likeness to other individuals (Thaler and Sunstein 2008, 96). As is now apparent, this method has been perfected in the recommender systems used not only on Netflix but also on social media platforms like Facebook, which use complex algorithmic processes to evaluate different options and personalize them for every user.[5] It is also no surprise that these new capabilities for better and more individual targeting have brought huge changes to the advertisement industry. As examined by Joseph Turow, in the current digital landscape Facebook has a significant role in giving advertisers the capability to better target advertisements based on things like online behaviors, past purchases, and locational data (Turow 2011). As Turow notes, Facebook has become one of the central gatekeepers of this information, and advertisers' access to the information relies on the use of Facebook's advertising tools, which are not free (Turow 2011, 138). In 2019 the total revenue of Facebook was $70,697 million, of which advertising revenue was $69,655 million (Facebook E). Advertising is Facebook's key source of revenue.

"Nudge is a curious mechanism, for it both presupposes and pushes against freedom; it assumes a choosing subject, but one who is constitutionally ill equipped to make rational, healthy choices," Natasha Dow Schüll and Caitlin Zaloom (2011, 523) write. Of course, not all work that describes nudge-like practices should be mapped out through nudge theory; online manipulation and persuasion, for example, constitute their own specific cases, which are slightly different than "nudging" (Susser, Roessler, and Nissenbaum 2019). Yet, the software-based capability to steer people's behavior by adjusting the parameters and features of digital environments plays well into its framework. Control of choice in nudge theory is premised on the capability to modify the environments in which choices take place. One of Thaler and Sunstein's examples involves a school cafeteria where fruit is placed in front of dessert to encourage consumption of healthy apples instead of less healthy sponge cakes (Thaler and Sunstein 2008, 1–3, 10). The authors maintain that this situation coerces no one to make any particular selection, but the placement of goods within the cafeteria makes certain choices easier than others. Apte, when analyzing Facebook as a choice architecture, reminds us that there are methods of nudging more refined than just placing things in certain order within the interface: her examples range from social nudges to algorithm-based hypernudges—in the former, users' Newsfeed posts influence others through network effects, and in the latter, recommendation algorithms select nudges based on, for example, predictive modeling (Apte 2020, 6; Yeung 2017). What is also important to Apte and, for example, Karen Yeung (2017), who writes about hypernudges, is that some nudges induce passive behaviors while others activate them. In the following section, I will explore the nudges of the Off-Facebook Activity tool by examining how it is introduced as part of the Facebook interface and how it is positioned within its environment. Central here is the notion of "default" and how Facebook's settings enable the choice of certain selections instead of others.

Defaults

As described in the instructional video featuring Meera and David, the Off-Facebook Activity tool lets users see a summary of the apps and websites that by default are allowed to send Facebook information about their activity (Facebook D). If users so choose, they can clear this information from their accounts. First, they must access their Facebook settings, and then click on "Off-Facebook Activity," which will present options to "Manage your Facebook Activity" or "Clear History" (Facebook D). The "Manage" option provides a list of businesses from which off-Facebook activity is gathered. The tool offers a clean list-based interface where the user chooses to either remove off-Facebook activity partly by individually selecting which website and app is given access or clearing the entire off-Facebook history with one button. If users choose to turn off future activity, this selection will be activated within 48 hours and their past activity will also be erased (Facebook F). By clicking the individual selection, such as the hypothetical Tom's Backpacks, the user enters a page that gives general details about how Facebook has received this information and the number of interactions received. The user can then choose to go to the advertiser's website, disconnect the link between that particular off-Facebook website, or give feedback about the reported activity.

The tool's functionality is based on what nudge theorists call "choice architecture" (Thaler and Sunstein 2008, 3), whereby individuals are also assigned a default position and "digital decision-guidance processes" inform their default settings (Yeung 2017, 121).[6] By default the off-Facebook activity is not blocked. According to nudge theory, defaults are particular nudges that take place in moments when what happens below the threshold of user's awareness becomes amplified. In these moments, defaults guide our choices. Far beyond software operations, defaults represent a widespread cultural phenomenon. Eric Johnson and Daniel Goldstein discuss the impact of defaults on medicine and organ donation, where making the default to opt in or opt out significantly affects the number of donations (Johnson and Goldstein 2003). Another classic example from behavioral economics is the default to opt in or out of a retirement plan (Choi et al. 2004). Defaults may enable choices but they also indicate that certain choices are privileged over others (Shah and Kesan 2008, 990). According to Johnson and Goldstein, defaults can influence choices in three ways: they imply a recommended action; they reduce the effort needed in decision making; and they "often represent the existing state or status quo, and change usually involves a trade-off" (Johnson and Goldstein 2003, 1338).

In complex choice situations defaults can be used to guide the decision-making process without forcing the user to choose (Thaler, Sunstein, and Balz 2013, 431). The choice to do nothing is to choose the default. Important here is that choosing to do nothing seems to be the users' default state. For example, Rajiv Shah and Christian Sandvig's research shows that when users configure their Wi-Fi settings most do not change their default settings at all (2008, 41). "For reasons of laziness, fear, and distraction, many people will take whatever option requires the least effort, or the path of least resistance," Thaler, Sunstein, and Balz (2013) observe. Thaler maintains that "behavioral tendencies toward doing nothing will be reinforced if the default option comes with some implicit or explicit suggestion that it represents the normal or even the recommended course of action" (Thaler, Sunstein and Balz 2013, 430).

Users might be the best persons to control their data, but that does not mean that they do so. Shah and Sandvig assert that the power to regulate users' behavior on the internet is in the hands not of individuals or legislators but those "who set software defaults" (2008, 26). While the meanings of "defaults," "settings," and "configurations" differ slightly in computer science, legal contexts, and software studies, the consensus remains that they should not be taken lightly. Defaults are not only at the core of the user experience of software-based choice architectures but also expressive of power relations. José van Dijck claims that "Facebook has every interest in preserving its default settings that make information as open as possible" (van Dijck 2013, 53). Apte notes that Facebook's privacy settings at least up until recently have been set open to allow the free expansion of connectivity (2020, 5). Vaidhyanathan argues further that companies like Facebook may claim to empower us by giving us choices, but simultaneously they set the defaults of connectivity in their favor (2018, 74). Defaults create an illusion of control, a placebo effect of sorts (Vaccaro et al. 2018).

When writing about Facebook's default settings as nudges, Apte notes that "either a user can be prompted to act, or she/he can be lulled into inaction depending on what benefits the platform." By giving the users the Off-Facebook Activity tool and an architecture through which the user can make their Facebook experience more private, the platform provides the user with an explicit form of control. However, the tool is also surrounded with what Apte calls as a "passivity-inducing nudge" (Apte 2020, 7–8): the user needs to take additional steps to use the tool and turn off-Facebook Activity off. The tool is buried in user's privacy settings and by default off-Facebook activity is always turned on. Adjusting off-Facebook Activity settings—and even becoming aware of the existence of these choices—demands conscious action. The off-Facebook Activity is on by default—both literally and metaphorically.

"There is no simple solution to the problem of privacy, because privacy itself is a solution to societal challenges that are in constant flux," Finn Brunton and Helen Nissenbaum (2015, 98) write. Vaidhyanathan argues that things like privacy are always subordinate to Facebook's business model, which is based on capturing users' data and attention "to give us [users] more of what we tell Facebook we want and to help advertisers precisely match their pleas for commerce with those who might be interested in those goods and services" (Vaidhyanathan 2018, 76). In the following sections I will claim that while the Off-Facebook Activity tool provides users with autonomy and explicit control, the passivity-inducing nudges are in place to mitigate the potential financial harms stricter privacy settings can cause for the platform. Central here is how Facebook defines the off-Facebook space and the relation advertisers and targeted advertising have with the platform.

Off-Facebook

When the makers of the Off-Facebook Activity tool note that the best persons to be in control of data are users themselves, they imply that individual users have the knowledge of "good" and "bad" data practices and that they already understand the importance of privacy. The point of criticism here is that instead of changing its core business model, Facebook keeps finding other means to tackle privacy issues.[7] The choice architecture the company provides for its users via the Off-Facebook Activity tool may serve to redirect human behavior toward more private use of social media, but this nudging does not substantially alter the wider sociopolitical, cultural, or economic online environment, which remains based on unrestricted flows of information instead of privacy (cf. Pedwell 2017, 80). Arguably, the structural problems related to data privacy are left untouched for a reason: advertising income.

"As of late 2018," according to statistics cited by Anne Helmond, David Nieborg, and Fernando van der Vlist, "Facebook hosted over 90 million businesses and 6 million active advertisers" (2019, 123). The sheer economic influence of these "third parties" illustrates why critics like Vaidhyanathan (2018, 9–10) have argued that the company and its product have grown too large to control: "Facebook is too big, too powerful, and too intrusive—and it works too well—for shallow reform to make a difference." The platform's growth is a result of what Nick Couldry and Ulises A. Mejias (2019, xii) describe as "data colonialism," a concept for how information technologies and "new infrastructures of connection" are "woven into" people's daily lives and practices. Facebook's power is predicated on the way it has spread and found its way into online spaces (see also Karppi 2018).

While the Off-Facebook Activity tool can be used to analyze how the company frames data control as an individual responsibility, it can also be used to analyze the wider structural changes Facebook has brought to the networked environment. This outside, which Facebook calls "off-Facebook," has a very particular, exact definition in the context of its tool.

The production of something as the outside is telling of historical, material, social, and economic powers at play (Probyn 1996, 12). Off-Facebook space is constituted by the various entities such as advertisers and marketers in possession of websites and apps that can be connected to the Facebook platform but are not owned, built, or managed by the corporation itself. "Off-Facebook activity is a summary of activity that businesses and organizations share with us about your interactions with them, such as visiting their apps or websites," Facebook (Facebook F) tells us. One way to define off-Facebook space is thus to look more closely at advertisers' and marketers' role in the platform, especially how they actively create this role by connecting themselves to the platform. A description of this connective practice can be found in the recent works of Helmond, Nieborg, and their colleagues. Building the grounds for their approach, Helmond (2015, 1) explains Facebook's growth with the notion of platformization, which "entails the extension of social media platforms into the rest of the web and their drive to make external web data 'platform ready.'" For Helmond, what differentiates social media sites from platforms is their operative logic.

The logic of any platform involves "interoperability" in two interconnected senses: connecting everything within its system and appropriating all the different kinds of data those interconnections allow (Nieborg and Helmond 2019, 203). Like Couldry and Mejias, Nieborg and Helmond cite the intensification of this logic as the reason behind Facebook's economic growth and technological expansion. Arguing that platformization made Facebook into the infrastructure of connection, Helmond, Nieborg, and van der Vlist (2019, 141) claim that it has gained "infrastructural properties over time by accumulating external dependencies through computational and organisational platform integrations." In addition, Nieborg, Helmond, and van der Vlist trace how throughout its history, Facebook has expanded its boundaries, for example, through application programming interfaces (APIs) and software development kits (SDKs) that integrate different stakeholders into the platform. Taken together, these are what Facebook calls "business tools," which, in addition to APIs and SDKs, include "the Facebook Pixel, Facebook social plugins, such as the Like and Share buttons, Facebook Login and Account Kit, and other Platform integrations, as well as other plugins, code, specifications, documentation, technology and services" (Facebook G).

Facebook argues that its business tools allow the company to build a better user experience and businesses to improve their reach by more accurately targeting the "right" people (Facebook H). Adam Arvidsson explains that Facebook built a technology of social graphs to describe interactions (which it calls "edges") between not only individual users but also objects (which can be users but also other things) (Arvidsson 2016, 10). Facebook Pixel, for example, measures cross-device conversions, which means that if a web-store has integrated Pixel, it can determine whether a Facebook ad resulted in the purchase of goods on its site (Facebook I). This information is shared not only with the business but also with Facebook, constituting an example of off-Facebook activity.

In the platform's own definition of off-Facebook activity, it does not refer to anything fundamentally outside the platform but rather practices of connecting things with the platform. This off-Facebook space is specifically occupied by business partners who want to use Facebook for marketing. Off-Facebook activity represents a connection that takes place via the company's own business tools: "a summary of activity that businesses and organizations share with us about your interactions, such as visiting their apps or websites" (Facebook C). Business tools provide access to off-Facebook activity information, which can be utilized to show users more relevant ads, give recommendations for events and Marketplace items, help users discover brands and businesses, and even identify suspicious activity (Facebook C). Off-Facebook activity includes a variety of interactions, from opening apps and viewing content to making purchases or merely adding items to shopping carts (Facebook C). Activity can include actions involving "apps and websites you've logged into with Facebook" as well as "data service providers and marketing agencies" (Facebook C). The logic governing how certain ads appear on particular users' screens is tied to how the off-Facebook space is technically connected to the Facebook platform and turned into flows of information. Significantly, clearing one's off-Facebook activity history does not delete the information but only unlinks these information sources from one's individual account (Facebook A).[8] If a user chooses to disconnect their off-Facebook activity, the number of ads they see will remain the same, but they should no longer be personalized. To be sure, ads for anything from backpacks to dating services will continue to appear in everyone's Facebook account, only they would not be based on user activity derived from off-Facebook sites.

One of the main sources of Facebook's power, according to José van Dijck, Nieborg, and Thomas Poell, (2019, 8) is its interrelational and dynamic structure, which I see expressed in the relationship between off-Facebook and, for lack of a better term, "on-Facebook," both of which are really just Facebook. In the discourses of the Off-Facebook Activity tool, the company's own rhetoric asserts that other businesses, apps, and websites constitute the off-Facebook space, but it is important to reiterate that Facebook's business model is contingent to these edges in their network. What Facebook describes as off-Facebook space is not an *absolute outside*; it is not completely distinct or disconnected from the platform but rather immanent or connected. As the hyphen in the name suggests, off-Facebook space is elementally conjoined, combined, and linked with Facebook in theory—and, in practice, with APIs and SDKs. It is not the negation of Facebook, since off-Facebook advertisers remain integral to the platform. The off-Facebook is constitutive to the entire existence of the platform: off-Facebook companies not only financially support the platform in the form of revenue; their objects form edges and build Facebook's social graphs by bringing information to the company from across different platforms and services. Off-Facebook for Facebook gives the platform its structure and grounds its limits. From this perspective, it is clear why for each individual user the off-Facebook environment is not *off* by default.

Debt

At first glance, the Off-Facebook Activity tool may appear to be a simple choice architecture related to controlling one's privacy; but the actual choice that is being nudged can be found elsewhere. The promotional and informational videos for the Off-Facebook Activity tool show the importance of the connection between third-party businesses and the social platform. For individual users, the discourses surrounding the tool rationalize the company's practices of personalized targeted marketing and devalue privacy in favor of the delivery of "better," "more accurate," "more interesting" content.

To stress the importance of advertisers to the platform, a voice-over in a video "Why Do Ads Feel Like They Are Directed to You, Personally?" (Facebook J), that appears in the tool's promotional materials as additional reference, explains that "advertising has become more tailored. More personal. And that's more effective because people prefer ads that are relevant to them." Significantly, the voiceover also emphasizes that "this creates incentives for advertisers to make ads that are truly tailored to people's interests. And these ads are what helped make the most of the Internet free" (Facebook J). The implication is that if users stop receiving targeted ads from Facebook (by for example using the Off-Facebook Activity tool), not only will their experience suffer, but the existence of the whole platform will be at risk. The second informational video "Where Online Advertising Is Headed," which also appears as reference material for the Off-Facebook Activity tool, uses almost the exact same language:

> Turns out people would rather see ads for things they like. And because the web's revenue model is mostly ad supported, seeing ads means you can use services like search engines and social media free of charge. It is important for ads to feel relevant because if they aren't, then people won't click on them. And if they don't click, businesses won't find them valuable and won't want to advertise on the web, which means *no more free web.* (Facebook K; emphasis added.)

While the company may provide users with tools to control their privacy, it hardly encourages them to do so in the promotional discourses. The rhetoric of the "free web" in these videos entices users to accept the defaults of the Off-Facebook Activity tool. The nudge here is that Facebook is only free because *users let the outside in*; users are allegedly doing themselves a favor when they let the company connect them to businesses and serve up targeted advertisements based on their personal Facebook profiles.

This perspective of course is hardly new. Susanna Paasonen (2018) points out that data, time, and attention are the price paid for a "free" Facebook. Although Paasonen builds productively on criticism that using Facebook's platform can be considered in terms of a market where users exchange commodities with the platform, the promotional materials for the Off-Facebook Activity tool provide another way to think about our engagement with the platform.

Let me return to the term "default," which according to the *Oxford English Dictionary* has additional meanings that cannot be reduced to technology settings: "failure to do something required or expected," especially the "failure to appear in court" or the "failure to meet financial commitments."[9] Adopting this additional sense of defaults can sharpen our analysis of Facebook user relation in terms of debt. In this model, users do not exchange commodities with the platform but offer repayments for the bond issued between Facebook and themselves. The important difference here is that exchange relation operates through temporary dynamics—entities enter and exit exchanges freely—but for the debt-relation there is no exit or outside until the debt has been paid. As a mode of engagement, debt is thus always more binding than an exchange.

Facebook can be interpreted as a debt market in both financial and moral senses. Facebook's nudges in the promotional and instructional videos include an emotional appeal that users owe the platform their information. First, the videos imply that, given that the platform is "free," users should not think about it as a business but as a favor; anyone who signs up carries this debt of gratitude. If users are taken to owe the platform, the best way for them to repay it is to refrain from adjusting their off-Facebook activity settings or disconnecting their Facebook accounts. In return for the platform's services, users are expected to pay their dues by accepting not only targeted ads but the company's entire advertisement-based business model—because without these things, social platforms would apparently lose their revenue and fold.

The debt relation also relies on the idea that the users consciously or unconsciously are trying to avert their losses. To this end, the discourses surrounding the Off-Facebook Activity tool underscore the disadvantages of using tools to restrict data flows: some may be personal, affecting the quality of users' everyday experience of the platform; others may be collective, as in the company's assertion that a "free web" is contingent on targeted marketing. Mobilizing a familiar "slippery slope" argument, Facebook's rhetoric of the Off-Facebook Activity tool presents a single user's seemingly "free choice" or to disconnect as a threat to everyone.

What is at stake here is the users "right to disconnect" (Hesselberth 2018, 1995, 2006). It would be an overinterpretation to claim that this set of nudges, which highlight the importance of targeted marketing for Facebook and places the entire model of the free web at risk, are intentionally placed to manipulate the users not to use the tool. Rather, what we see here is that for Facebook nothing can exist outside this model of connectivity without also being destructive for their business. Hence folding everything inside and keeping it there becomes of crucial importance to the extent that the outside of connectivity gradually disappears.

Outside

"The problem always has the solution it deserves," as Gilles Deleuze (1991, 16) puts it, "in terms of the way in which it is stated (i.e. the conditions under which it is determined as problem), and of the means and terms at our disposal for stating it." The same can be said of the Off-Facebook Activity tool: its discourses show that the "problems" of privacy as they are defined by the company exclude the material conditions of the platform and the business model built around effective, data-based targeted marketing. These two defaults remain unchanged. Presenting the tool as a "solution" for more than two billion active Facebook users is like suggesting a band-aid for a bullet wound. It may stop a drip of leaky data here and there, but it does not change the business model that relies on its unobstructed circulation.

In place of a conclusion, I argue that a theorization of *the problem of the outside* can open a new vector for thinking about disconnection beyond the Off-Facebook Activity tool and the nudges it encapsulates. The Off-Facebook Activity tool presents solutions that are only applicable for the user who is already within the system, and the same applies to the nudge theory. "At the end of the day," Pedwell (2017, 80–81) asserts, "nudge theory's focus is on changing *individual behavior* (through superficial modifications of administrative arrangements and other choice architectures) rather than enacting deeper social or structural changes, or, indeed, understanding the complex and shifting interactions among bodies, infrastructures and environments." Mona Mannevuo (2019, 35), who explores the use of nudges in the context of universal basic income experiments, points out that for the theory, freedom of the choice is an illusion: "people are free to make choices—as long as they make choices within the post-bureaucratic choice architecture constructed by the state." If nudge theory remains focused on managing how fruits, desserts, and sponge cakes are organized in a cafeteria, then it can fall far short of changing nutrition standards and meal requirements on a more comprehensive level. If nudge theory is primarily about tweaking opt-ins and opt-outs for the retirement system, then it might foreclose the possibility of rethinking pension as a whole. When Facebook designs a feature that disconnects for a more private user experience, that disconnection still happens safely within the parameters of the platform.

Jenny Sundén and Jelisaveta Blagojević's (2019, 57) note that "breaks and disruptions," force us to think "what it means to connect, or to relate, in the first place." What I have tried to address in this chapter, in contrast, is the importance of understanding what you *disconnect to* when you use the Off-Facebook Activity tool. One could be reminded here that the word "disconnect" consists of two parts: *dis-* meaning "the opposite of" and the root, *connect,* is based on a Latin verb *connectere,* which has two parts: *con-* (together) + *nectere* (bind), as in "to join together." While contemporary disconnection studies have focused heavily on showing that disconnection is a meaningful act in its apparent opposition to connection, what has evaded attention is the question of what becomes joined together in the act of disconnecting: what is the outside that is affirmed and finds its shape in disconnection?

One of the theorists interested in this question is Hesselberth, whose structuring paradox of disconnection is inspired by the notion of the "constitutive outside" by Chantal Mouffe, who in turn takes it from Jacques Derrida (Hesselberth 2018, 2007). According to Mouffe (2005, 15), the constitutive outside explains how the creation of identity is relational and contingent to "the establishment of difference, difference which is often constructed on the basis of hierarchy, for example between form and matter, black and white, man and woman, etc." This is the difference users find if they activate their Off-Facebook Activity tool. By developing the tool, the company develops an artificial opposition between the inside and outside, between the platform and the marketers. The user disconnects their personal data flows from marketers and advertisers, but this is only a partial disconnect. The user does not disconnect from Facebook or even its fundamental form of business practice; as repeated by the promotional materials, the user will still see ads. The user is still within the reach of marketers and advertisers who with software developer kits and APIs are part of the platform.

The outside that Facebook designs and delimits with the tool takes a form that resembles the inside and thus corresponds to the conditions under which it is being designed.[10] Privacy does not mean being free from targeting, the difference is in how personalized it is. Thus, when disconnecting their off-Facebook activity users do not end up in the outside but rather find themselves being in the *offside*. This offside is immanent to the "rules of the game" and has a specified function within the system: the offside is Facebook with less personalized content. The difference the tool produces is only a difference in degree in which users are exploited and thus does not have much to do with a more structural qualitative change.[11] The offside masked as the outside is not the negation of connection.

Hesselberth (2018, 2007) argues that the constitutive outside forces us to see the limits of connectivity and hence offers a point of resistance to the claims that there is "'no outside' to our 'current culture of connectivity.'" The off-Facebook taken as the offside, in contrast, indicates that even the outside, at least partly, can be connected and captured by the logic of connectivity. In this sense, the offside seems to be a manifestation of what Taina Bucher (2020, 611) means when she says that practices of opting out and even refusals to connect are nothing but forms of connection and "there is nothing to disconnect from in the digital world" (610). What Bucher with this claim seeks for is not to refute the acts of disconnection completely, but to find new ways to articulate what being-with the outside means (615–16).

Keith Ansell-Pearson (1999, 84) writes that "it is the forces of the 'outside' which impinge and impact upon us, upon what we think we are and what we think we are capable of becoming." If off-Facebook is the outside at the user's reach, there is very little liberation in the act of disconnecting. If everyone retains the given choice architectures or keeps on only nudging this or that, they will never change the whole system. It should be noted, however, that Pearson in the quote above is referring to Deleuze's understanding of the outside instead of Derrida's or Mouffe's. The implication of this perspective is that the outside should not be conceived through opposition or negation. In the Deleuzean reading, the incipience of resistance resides with disconnection but only if, as a solution, it begins from the acknowledgment that the outside exists external to its relation with Facebook.[12]

My examination of Facebook and off-Facebook shows that the relations between online and offline, Facebook and off-Facebook, inside and outside perform specific functions for the company. Off-Facebook and on-Facebook are both based on a specific imaginary of the outside that is functional. The function of this imaginary is to define the relation of being-with Facebook. Either we are immersed fully with the Facebook experiences and the features and functions that constitute it, or our experience is limited by the disconnected off-Facebook activity. In both cases, the insides and the outsides belong to Facebook and are being defined by them. Yet, an outside that cannot be undone exists. The world, the offline, even the free internet exists independently to any particular imaginary or manifestation of social media. There is always something we can *disconnect to.* As Ansell-Pearson (1999, 84) notes, "It is the peristaltic movements of the outside which serve to destratify fixed and stable identities and produce through doubling processes new possibilities for an intenser and more creative existence." What disconnection studies needs are not only different theories of relations but also ways to find the outside.

Notes

1 Transcribed by the author.

2 The same video is also featured on "What Is Off-Facebook Activity?" website (Facebook C).

3 This is the so-called endowment effect (Kahneman, Knetsch, and Thaler 1991, 194).

4 Choice is a central notion in the emerging field of nudge theory. This theory is credited to Richard Thaler and Cass Sunstein. Thaler was awarded the Nobel Prize in Economics in 2017 for his work in behavioral economics.

5 On social media, personalization, as done by current algorithmic media systems and understood as a nudge, uses data on users' connections, habits, and preferences to predict the choices that become available for them. Karen Yeung calls algorithmically personalized nudges "hypernudges," because they are "networked," "continuously updated," "dynamic," "pervasive," potent and thus powerful (Yeung 2017). The Off-Facebook Activity tool, however, is much more traditional in its operations.

6 Yang Wang et al. (2014) have suggested that privacy nudges designed specifically for the Facebook user interface can help users "consider the content and audience of their online disclosures more carefully" and avoid regretting making Facebook posts. One example of the privacy nudges they designed is a feature that shows the audience reacting to a Facebook post before it is posted and then delays posting it with a visible countdown timer, giving the user time to delete the message after hitting the send button but before the audience sees it. The nudge here is not textual but based on Facebook's user-interface design and provides a visual aid for decision making. Implementation of this nudge would also change the default action when the user hits the send button from an instant to a delayed response. The takeaway is that the user interface is designed in a certain way and should not be taken as given. Furthermore, as Yeung points out, software-based algorithmic choice architecture can be continuously reconfigured and optimized (Yeung 2017, 122).

7 In 2018, the European Union's General Data Protection Regulation (GDPR) came into effect. Its purpose was to establish requirements for businesses operating with user data to keep the data protected and give EU citizens more control over their data. The off-Facebook Activity tool can be seen as one of Facebook's responses to the GDPR (Ready 2019).

8 As described in the promotional materials (Facebook A): "The information you disconnect will no longer be connected to your account. This data can still be used without being linked to an individual user to allow us [Facebook] to let businesses know how their website, app, or ads are performing."

9 "Default." *Oxford English Dictionary.* Accessed April 27, 2020. https://www.oed.com/view/Entry/48723?rskey=x83Jjk&result=1#eid.

10 What I am paraphrasing here is Deleuze's take on the relation of solution and problem but also his criticism of understanding difference through resemblance (Deleuze 2004).

11 See here Deleuze's (2004, 299–300) discussion between the difference in degree and difference in kind.

12 Deleuze in *Dialogues II* famously argues that "relations are external to their terms" and "relations may change without the terms changing" (Deleuze and Parnet 2007, 55). Hence, we should not think the terms or the relations independently but together (56). Here I am also in debt to Levi Bryant, who in a blog post interprets Deleuze and argues that "insofar as relations are external to their terms, insofar as objects are independent of their relations, where relations exist we can begin with the assurance that these relations were *built* or *constructed*" (Bryant 2011).

References

Acquisti, Alessandro. 2009. "Nudging Privacy: The Behavioral Economics of Personal Information." *IEEE Security & Privacy* 7:82–85.

Acquisti, Alessandro, Leslie K. John, and George Loewenstein. 2013. "What Is Privacy Worth?" *Journal of Legal Studies* 42:249–74.

Ansell-Pearson, Keith. 1999. *Germinal Life.* London: Routledge.

Apte, Deepti Singh. 2020. "Explicit Autonomy, Implicit Control: User Autonomy in the Dichotomous Choice Architecture of Facebook." *Journal of Creative Communications:* 1–12. Accessed April 27, 2020. https://doi.org/10.1177/0973258619893787.

Arvidsson, Adam. 2016. "Facebook and Finance: On the Social Logic of the Derivative." *Theory, Culture & Society* 33, no. 6: 3–23.

Brunton, Finn, and Helen Nissenbaum. 2015. *Obfuscation: A User's Guide for Privacy and Protest.* Cambridge, Mass.: MIT Press.

Bryant, Levi. 2011. "Forging Relations." *Larval Subjects,* January 24. Accessed April 27, 2020. https://larvalsubjects.wordpress.com/2011/01/24/forging-relations/.

Bucher, Taina. 2020. "Nothing to Disconnect From? Being Singular Plural in an Age of Machine Learning." *Media, Culture & Society* 42, no. 4: 610–17.

Choi, James J., David Laibson, Brigitte C. Madrian, and Andrew Metrick. 2004. "For Better or for Worse: Default Effects and 401(k) Savings Behavior." In *Perspectives on the Economics of Aging,* ed. David A. Wise, 81–125. Chicago: University of Chicago Press.

Chun, Wendy Hui Kyong. 2016. *Updating to Remain the Same: Habitual New Media.* Cambridge, Mass.: MIT Press.

Couldry, Nick, and Ulises A. Mejias. 2019. *The Costs of Connection. How Data Is Colonizing Human Life and Appropriating It for Capitalism.* Stanford, Calif.: Stanford University Press.

Deleuze, Gilles. 1991. *Bergsonism.* New York: Zone Books.

Deleuze, Gilles. 2004. *Difference and Repetition.* London: Continuum.

Deleuze, Gilles, and Claire Parnet. 2007. *Dialogues II.* New York: Columbia University Press.

Dow Schüll, Natasha, and Caitlin Zaloom. 2011. "The Shortsighted Brain: Neuroeconomics and the Governance of Choice in Time." *Social Studies of Science* 41, no. 4: 515–38.

Draper, Nora A. 2019. *The Identity Trade. Selling Privacy and Reputation Online.* New York: New York University Press.

Facebook A. "The Best Person to Be in Control of Data Is You." Facebook. Accessed April 24, 2020. https://www.facebook.com/off-facebook-activity.

Facebook B. "How Do I Disconnect My Off-Facebook Activity?" Facebook Help Center. Accessed April 20, 2020. https://www.facebook.com/help/287199741901674?helpref=search&sr=2&query=off-facebook&search_session_id=7d6cdfaa572cea7249af9761d4023ae5.

Facebook C. "What Is Off-Facebook Activity?" Facebook Help Center. Accessed April 20, 2020. https://www.facebook.com/help/2207256696182627.

Facebook D. "Meer Introduces Our New Data Control to Her Husband," on "The Best Person to Be in Control of Data Is You," Facebook. Accessed April 24, 2020. https://www.facebook.com/off-facebook-activity.

Facebook E. "Facebook Reports Fourth Quarter and Full Year 2019 Results" Facebook Investor Relations. Accessed April 27, 2020. https://investor.fb.com/investor-news/press-release-details/2020/Facebook-Reports-Fourth-Quarter-and-Full-Year-2019-Results/default.aspx.

Facebook F. "How Do I Manage My Future Off-Facebook Activity?" Facebook Help Center. Accessed January 28, 2020. https://www.facebook.com/help/1224342157705160?helpref=faq_content.

Facebook G. "The Facebook Business Tools." Facebook Help Center. Accessed January 28, 2020. https://www.facebook.com/help/331509497253087?helpref=faq_content.

Facebook H. "How Does Facebook Receive Information from Other Businesses and Organizations?" Facebook Help Center. Accessed January 28, 2020. https://www.facebook.com/help/2230503797265156?helpref=faq_content.

Facebook I. "The Facebook Pixel." Facebook for Business. Accessed January 28, 2020. https://www.facebook.com/business/learn/facebook-ads-pixel.

Facebook J. "Why Do Ads Feel Like They Are Directed to You, Personally?" on "The Best Person to Be in Control of Data Is You." Facebook. Accessed April 24, 2020. https://www.facebook.com/off-facebook-activity.

Facebook K. "Where Online Adverstising Is Headed," on "The Best Person to Be in Control of Data Is You," Facebook. Accessed April 24, 2020. https://www.facebook.com/off-facebook-activity.

Facebook L. "Introducing Off-Facebook Activity: A New Tool That Gives You More Control of Your Data," on "The Best Person to Be in Control of Data Is You," Facebook. Accessed April 24, 2020. https://www.facebook.com/off-facebook-activity.

Helmond, Anne. 2015. "The Platformization of the Web: Making Web Data Platform Ready." *Social Media + Society* 1, no. 2: 1–11. Accessed April 27, 2020. https://doi.org/10.1177/2056305115603080.

Helmond, Anne, David B. Nieborg, and Fernando N. van der Vlist. 2019. "Facebook's Evolution: Development of a Platform-as-Infrastructure." *Internet Histories* 3, no. 2: 123–46.

Hesselberth, Pepita. 2018. "Discourses on Disconnectivity and the Right to Disconnect." *New Media & Society* 20, no. 5: 1994–2010.

Johnson, Eric J., and Daniel Goldstein. 2003. "Do Defaults Save Lives?" *Science* 302 (5649): 1338–39.

Juzwiak, Rich. 2019. "Every Ad on My Computer Is Suddenly Ashley Madison." *Slate,* October 14. Accessed April 27, 2020. https://slate.com/human-interest/2019/10/ashley-madison-ads-on-computer-husband-cheating.html.

Kahneman, Daniel, Jack L. Knetsch, and Richard H. Thaler. 1990. "Experimental Tests of the Endowment Effect and the Coase Theorem." *Journal of Political Economy* 98:1325–48.

Kahneman, Daniel, Jack L. Knetsch, and Richard H. Thaler. 1991. "Anomalies. The Endowment Effect, Loss Aversion, and Status Quo Bias." *Journal of Economic Perspectives* 5, no. 1: 193–206.

Karppi, Tero. 2018. *Disconnect: Facebook's Affective Bonds.* Minneapolis: University of Minnesota Press.

Kokolakis, Spyros. 2017. "Privacy Attitudes and Privacy Behaviour: A Review of Current Research on the Privacy Paradox Phenomenon." *Computers & Security* 64:122–34.

Mannevuo, Mona. 2019. "Neuroliberalism in Action: The Finnish Experiment with Basic Income." *Theory, Culture & Society* 36, no. 4: 27–47.

Mouffe, Chantal. 2005. *On the Political.* London: Routledge.
Nieborg, David B., and Anne Helmond. 2019. "The Political Economy of Facebook's Platformization in the Mobile Ecosystem: Facebook Messenger as a Platform Instance." *Media, Culture & Society* 41, no. 2: 196–218.
Paasonen, Susanna. 2018. "Affect, Data, Manipulation and Price in Social Media." *Distinktion: Journal of Social Theory* 19, no. 2: 214–29. Accessed April 27, 2020. doi: 10.1080/1600910X.2018.1475289.
Pedwell, Carolyn. 2017. "Habit and the Politics of Social Change: A Comparison of Nudge Theory and Pragmatist Philosophy." *Body and Society* 23, no. 4: 59–94.
Probyn, Elspeth. 1996. *Outside Belongings.* New York: Routledge.
Ready, Frank. 2019. "Is 'Off-Facebook Activity' Privacy's Future or GDPR's Present?" *Law.com,* August 27. Accessed April 27, 2020. https://www.law.com/legaltech news/2019/08/27/is-off-facebook-activity-privacys-future-or-gdprs-present/?slre turn=20200028142833.
Shah, Rajiv C., and Jay P. Kesan. 2008. "Setting Online Policy with Software Defaults." *Information, Communication & Society* 11, no. 7: 989–1007.
Shah, Rajiv C., and Christian Sandvig. 2008. "Software Defaults as De Facto Regulation: The Case of the Wireless Internet." *Information, Communication & Society* 11, no. 1: 25–46.
Sundén, Jenny, and Jelisaveta Blagojević. 2019. "Dis/connections: Toward an Ontology of Broken Relationality." *Configurations* 27, no. 1: 37–57. Accessed April 27, 2020. doi:10.1353/con.2019.0001.
Susser, Daniel, Beate Roessler, and Helen Nissenbaum. 2019. "Online Manipulation: Hidden Influences in a Digital World." *Georgetown Law Technology Review.* 4, no. 1: 1–45.
Thaler, Richard H., and Cass R. Sunstein. 2003. "Libertarian Paternalism." *American Economic Review* 93, no. 2: 175–79.
Thaler, Richard H., and Cass R. Sunstein. 2008. *Nudge: Improving Decisions about Health, Wealth, and Happiness.* New Haven, Conn.: Yale University Press.
Thaler, Richard H., Cass R. Sunstein, and John P. Balz. 2013. "Choice Architecture." In *The Behavioral Foundations of Public Policy,* ed. Eldar Shafir, 428–39 Princeton, N.J.: Princeton University Press.
Turow, Joseph. 2011. *The Daily You: How the New Advertising Industry Is Defining Your Identity and Your Worth.* New Haven, Conn.: Yale University Press.
Vaccaro, Kristen, Dylan Huang, Motahhare Eslami, Christian Sandvig, Kevin Hamilton, and Karrie Karahalios. 2018. "The Illusion of Control: Placebo Effects of Control Settings. Paper 16." In *Proceedings of the 2018 CHI Conference on Human Factors in Computing Systems (CHI '18).* New York: ACM.
Vaidhyanathan, Siva. 2018. *Antisocial Media: How Facebook Disconnects Us and Undermines Democracy.* Oxford: Oxford University Press.
Van Dijck, José. 2013. *The Culture of Connectivity: A Critical History of Social Media.* Oxford: Oxford University Press.
Van Dijck, José, David B. Nieborg, and Thomas Poell. 2019. "Reframing Platform Power." *Internet Policy Review* 8, no. 2: 2–18.
Wang, Yang, Pedro Giovanni Leon, Alessandro Acquisti, Lorrie Faith Cranor, Alain

Forget, and Norman Sadeh. 2014. "A Field Trial of Privacy Nudges for Facebook." In *Proceedings of the SIGCHI Conference on Human Factors in Computing Systems (CHI '14)*, 2367–76. New York: ACM. Accessed April 27, 2020. http://dx.doi.org/10.1145/2556288.2557413.

Yeung, Karen. 2017. "'Hypernudge': Big Data as a Mode of Regulation by Design." *Information, Communication & Society* 20 (1): 118–36. Accessed April 2020, 27. doi: 10.1080/1369118X.2016.1186713.

[4]

Glossary

Clara Wieghorst and Lea P. Zierott

The equivocality of disconnection calls for collecting and assembling the different ways disconnection is understood across different disciplines, practices, and media technologies. Hardly a fully developed concept, let alone a coherent research field, disconnection is more like a placeholder for discussions about leaving networks, cutting connections, and refusing to be part of something. The following entries contain several examples of negative prefixes (un-, dis-, and de-), which we suggest seeing as positive practices of undoing networks. "In lieu of a conclusion," as Brian Massumi titles the last chapter of his book *Politics of Affect* (2015), this glossary does not aim to present an overview of established theoretical concepts but to pose better problems. Thus, this glossary makes no claim to completeness but can be understood as a playful attempt at mapping practices of undoing networks.

Even though disconnection discourses are equivocal (Hesselberth 2018), there are some recurrent strands of argumentation. Public discourses on disconnection often presume the existence of some state or space free of any media: "the analog," "irl" (in real life), or "offline," which are contrasted with "the digital," "virtual," or "online" environments that encompass everything computerized. To break with this digital dualism (Jurgenson 2013), this glossary presents a mapping of phenomena of undoing networks that pose better problems, such as pointing to the paradox of dis/connectivity

(Hesselberth 2018; Karppi 2018) or arguing that "the analog," far from being natural, needs to be constructed (Stäheli and Stoltenberg 2020). While some discourses of disconnection are linked to a neoliberal agenda of self-responsibilization, other movements or artistic practices aim to disrupt platform capitalism. The question of undoing networks is not merely a technical problem but a social and political one. Organizing the entries as interconnected sociopolitical phenomena rather than isolated theoretical concepts or names of celebrated authors should call attention to how disconnection is embedded in our everyday lives.

Analog Nostalgia

One epiphenomenon arising from the ubiquity of digital media is nostalgia for what are commonly known as "analog media" (Marks 2012; Schrey 2014). In media studies, the distinction between "digital" and "analog" remains contentious (Sterne 2016; Peters 2016). In everyday usage, however, analog media are defined quite simply as anything that is not computerized.[1] Living an "analog life" has become an entire trend. From analog photography to collecting and listening to vinyl records, from analog travel guides to coloring books for grown-ups, there is a whole range of activities and products that allow one to pursue "offline" hobbies.

Analog nostalgists feel that disconnecting from digital media and engaging with analog media enhances their lives. They experience the elaborate process of analog photography as rewarding; they like the "authentic" sound of vinyl. Analog nostalgists feel that traveling without Google Maps encourages them to talk to strangers and enhances their knowledge of foreign places. Ironically, there are digital apps like Hipstamatic, which aim to apply the aesthetics of analog photography to digital pictures taken with smartphones. Thus, analog nostalgia is hardly restricted to "old media" and can also be lived out via "new media." Significantly, the category of analog media was only created with the emergence of digital media, since it was not previously necessary to differentiate between the two modes.

Analog nostalgia does refer to more than the use of analog media. Especially within critical discourses on social media platforms, the adjective is increasingly used as a noun: "the analog" describes a pristine state or a space free of any media. The analog promises a more authentic and more human connection than found on social media. Ironically, a media theoretical adjective is used to describe a purportedly nonmedial condition. Stäheli and Stoltenberg (2020) describe the extensive work that goes into the construction of "the analog," drawing on case studies from digital detox tourism. They call this process of creating supposedly media-free zones "analogization," which turns out to be a heavily mediated process. The analog has to be created through the use of media including books, maps, or typewriters.

Break

In the context of disconnection, the "break" represents a conceptual category in theoretical research and a common theme in popular discourses calling for disconnection. Relating the break to affect theory, Jenny Sundén (2018) points to its disruptive and heuristic functions. To actualize "the queer potentials" (2018, 64) of the break, Sundén highlights moments of disconnectivity that potentially can open up new modes of relationality. The break's heuristic function consists in its ability "to bring forth what constant connectivity means, and how it feels" (64).

In popular discourses on disconnection, it is often argued that we need to take a break, whether it be from constantly looking at our phones, from refreshing our feeds on social media, or from following the news. While digital detox holidays promise a break from ubiquitous connectivity, the pursuit of analog hobbies claims to create a break from our digitally organized everyday lives. In this sense, digital connectivity is a state from which we need to take a break, whereas the break itself is a state that is necessarily free from digital media. Realistically, however, we often use the internet to take a break from other activities such as work or socializing. For many people, watching YouTube videos or shopping online can be relaxing, even rewarding activities after an exhausting day at the office. For others, the fact that they require typing and looking at a screen makes these leisure activities hardly distinguishable from work.

When standing awkwardly at a bus stop or in the corner of a room at a party, your smartphone can save you from making small talk. Checking social media or dating apps—or, in many cases, pretending to check them—might help introverts feel sociable and look busy at the same time. But as discourses on disconnection become increasingly popular, staring at your phone might also be dismissed as antisocial behavior. Comparing smartphones or the internet to cigarettes evokes not only a sense of addiction but also of breaks. Smoking a cigarette allows one to take a break from work and to *do* something at a party (as opposed to looking forlorn and self-conscious). Whereas smoking was once seen as a legitimate—even cool—activity, it is now widely considered to be unhealthy and irresponsible. The same holds true for smartphones along a much shorter span of time: they used to be fancy devices one could brag about (as is still possible in particular contexts) but their popularity is steadily declining. However, smartphone breaks and smoking breaks might differ in terms of their organizational effects. In cigarette breaks, it is possible that "relationships [between smokers are] being formed that would otherwise not occur" (Brewis and Grey 2008, 981), since people from different hierarchical positions have the chance to meet. What kinds of relationships might be formed among those who are taking a break from their phones and among those who are taking a break on their phones meeting on the Internet?

Dead Zones

As a gap in a comprehensive connection, the "dead zone" appears mostly as a problem—as something that needs to be eliminated. There are a variety of different technologies for finding and reporting places without (cellular or internet) coverage. There are also apps, like White Spots, that reinterpret the dead zone in positive terms. If you press the "get me out" button, you are guided to a map that shows "white spots" (i.e., places without coverage) around the world. Here you can find digital detox camps and hotels as well as phone-free cafés. In addition to these time-out places, the dead spot also represents a refuge for people who describe themselves as electromagnetic hypersensitive.

Since dead zones are often the result of a geographical disconnection that goes hand-in-hand with a digital one, they open up a spatial perspective: How is the dead zone spatially delimited and where do its borders lie? Usually caused by a lack of service or failure of infrastructure, there is no need for users to create dead zones. The practices that can be observed here therefore relate primarily to the organization of an already disconnected space.

To ask how dead zones occur raises questions about their technical foundation. Are dead zones actual holes in a horizontal, area-wide expansion of electromagnetic waves, or simply the result of a lack of radio and cellular towers? In fact, both are the case. In technical terms, a dead zone is an area in which the connection between transmitter and receiver is not possible, or only possible to create an insignificant degree of reception. This may be because the distance is simply too far or because the wave carrying the signal is intentionally interrupted or unintentionally disturbed. Transmission always depends on factors including atmosphere, weather influences, and the conductivity of the earth; additional disturbances or obstacles, such as roads, buildings, mountains, and narrow valleys, can further prevent the wave from propagating. Dead zones also occur when the radiation is absorbed by different objects. In addition to forests, the human body is another relatively large absorber, which can soak up certain kinds of radiation through the skin.

Besides these passive occurrences, the active creation of dead zones raises questions of power. Like many other countries, the U.S. government manages a huge area within which radio transmission is restricted for scientific research and military purposes. The National Radio Quiet Zone is a dead zone by law, divided into different zones according to the electronic devices that may be used there.

The question of mapping dead zones calls for alternative representations of networks. Mejias (2013) contests the logic of most network theories, which tend to focus on nodes, by concentrating on the spaces between them. The "paranodes" build a multidimensional space, which is located at the same time both inside and outside the network.

Digital Detox

The term "digital detox" describes a trend that seems to be inseparable from other current movements in support of mindfulness and healthism. People who take good care of themselves not only eat superfoods and practice yoga and meditation; they must also "unplug" from time to time in order to "recharge." Digital Detox® is the name of a company "focused on helping people be more present and improve the balance with technology use in their lives" (Digital Detox 2020).

The company's slogan is "Disconnect to Reconnect." Since 2012, Digital Detox® has hosted Camp Grounded®, a three-night adult summer camp where people travel to somewhere in California without an internet connection in order to "connect with one another, without devices" (Digital Detox 2020).[2] Campers can participate in what the organizers call "playshops." Separately, Digital Detox® arranges "unplugged nights out" in cities all over the United States where participants can meet new people without being distracted by their phones. Digital Detox® also funds research on the impact of technology and offers a certification to schools for combatting phone overuse among children and teenagers.

As a result of digital detox, phone use, or more generally "the digital," is toxified (Sutton 2017). Among many other scholars, Adam

Fish (2017) has criticized the neoliberal attempt to make individuals take responsibility for facing the impositions of capitalism and then selling them expensive products and packages to help them to get fit.

The underlying premise of the company's philosophy—and by now its numerous imitators—is its distinction between "good" and "bad" connections. The idea is that human beings feel a natural urge to connect with one another, a desire that cannot be satisfied by connecting via technological devices. If phone overuse is taken to contain the risk of damaging our ability to connect, then, according to proponents of digital detox, we need to "disconnect to reconnect."

Digital Detox Beauty Products

According to some proponents of digital detox, phone overuse and too much "screen time" threatens both our (mental) health and our (physical) beauty (in a very holistic sense). To mitigate the damaging effects of spending hours on digital devices, people can buy pricy beauty products.

One German natural cosmetic brand sells an anti-blue-light facial oil that attempts to cash in on the popularity of blue-light blocking computer glasses. It contains the ingredient marigold, which protects the skin against blue-light radiation from screens. This blue light is said not only to damage cells and contribute to skin aging but also to be the dominant cause of eyestrain resulting from extended periods of screen usage. Even though all of these claims have been debunked by scientific research, an American cosmetic brand offers a digital detox bath soak that promises to relieve its users from "EMFs" (electric and magnetic fields) and to fight the "wired and tired" syndrome. In one Vancouver-based culture magazine's review of the soak, users are recommended to drink plenty of water and not to stay in the tub too long, because the "soak's job is to literally rid the body of toxins"—an "intense . . . purification process" (Markovinovic 2019).

Once out of the bath, one can use a mineral-rich digital detox face mist, which purports to reenergize its user and to protect the skin from screen fatigue. The product description markets the face mist as "indispensable for air travel, at work or when using computers and mobile devices" (Niche Beauty, n.d.).

These digital detox beauty products, all of which come in beautifully designed packaging, are perfect examples of how media nonconsumption (Portwood-Stacer 2013) and temporary disconnection (Jorge 2019) can be part of neoliberal consumer capitalism. Their marketing agenda is based on creating desire by spreading anxiety. The underlying argumentation is this: We live in a toxic environment and live unhealthily. Spending our days in big cities, on airplanes or working on screens has damaging effects on our skin and our overall health. But don't worry—by buying these products you can protect yourself from serious damage and rid your body of toxins.

Through discourse analysis of Instagram, Ana Jorge (2019) has shown how digital disconnection and interruption are reintegrated on social media in the form of lifestyle choices. A selfie posted from a digital detox bath clearly illustrates how commodified practices of disconnection have become part of our everyday digital lives.

Digital Minimalism

Participating in the larger minimalist revival, the title of Cal Newport's latest book is *Digital Minimalism* (2019). A follow-up to *Deep Work* (2016) and *How to Become a Straight-A Student* (2006), the self-help guide gives practical advice on how to live a fulfilled life by regaining control over technology. Digital minimalists are people who are able to enjoy "offline" activities like reading a book, listening to other people or taking a walk without feeling the constant urge to check their phones. They can enjoy social events without needing to document them on Instagram and keep track of the news without suffering from information overload.

As part of his efforts to teach readers how to become digital minimalists, Newport's "Study Hacks Blog" (2020) encourages his followers to take part in "The Analog January Challenge." Because quitting screen-based activities can only be enjoyable when engaging in analog alternatives, Newport suggests five commitments: *Read* (three to four books, no matter which ones); *Move* (go for a fifteen-minute walk every day, without one's phone); *Connect* (have a "real" conversation with twenty different people during the month); *Make* (find a hobby that requires interaction with the physical world); and *Join* (a local group of people that meets weekly).

Unlike radical renunciation, digital minimalism does not recommend deleting all of one's social media accounts or even living a life without technology. Rather, its aim is to help people live a better life by making them feel less dependent on their technology. Digital minimalism is about moderation. It does not have any political impetus such as criticizing surveillance capitalism or the impertinence of permanent availability. Rather, it is consistent with the neoliberal agenda of creating resilient individuals that take responsibility for their own (mental) health and work efficiency.

Digital Suicide

Seppukoo.com and the Web 2.0 Suicide Machine are two art projects analyzed in an article by Tero Karppi (2011) on "Digital Suicide." Established in 2009, they both offered a form of digital "death" on Facebook and other social media platforms. Over a decade later, these art projects may seem ancient. As Facebook lost its popularity, it became more common for users to delete their accounts and keep only those on Twitter and Instagram, which of course is now owned by Facebook. Nevertheless, both art projects can still be seen as early examples of artistic disconnection practices, as cases of tactical media aiming to disrupt dominant platform capitalism.

Each project works differently than strategies of digital minimalism or digital detox, which tend to aim at personal well-being rather than resistance. The rebellious character of Seppukoo (the name refers to a form of Japanese ritual suicide) and the Web 2.0 Suicide Machine is attested to by the fact that Facebook fought legal battles against each of them. For a brief period of time, Seppukoo.com announced that "due to the paradoxical controversy between the giant Facebook and Seppukoo, our suicidal services are now useless" (Seppukoo 2009). Alongside this announcement, there is a video of Japanese Samurais accompanied by voices speaking in Japanese (with English subtitles) telling the story of the website's demise.[3]

The Web 2.0 Suicide Machine no longer works either. Its services once operated by having Facebook users who were willing to commit digital suicide enter their Facebook username and password. While Seppukkoo would have then logged into the user's Facebook account and used their information to create a memorial page on Seppukoo.com, the Web 2.0 Suicide Machine would have simply changed the user's password so that they were not able to log into Facebook anymore. The user's profile picture would then have been changed into the Web 2.0 Suicide Machine logo, and their Facebook friends deleted one-by-one. This whole process happened automatically and was visible to the user. As Karppi puts it, "The Facebook life [sic!] is disappearing in front of the user's eyes" (2011, 10).

Disappearing

In her video installation "How Not to Be Seen," whose title reframes the classic Monty Python sketch of the same name, artist Hito Steyerl seeks more serious ways of becoming invisible. "Whatever is not captured by resolution is invisible" (Steyerl 2013) she states, suggesting several tactics of disappearance. As in the classic sketch, most of these tactics aim at becoming invisible in the sense of "not being part of a picture" and thus being unseen. Escaping the overall demand for transparency is seen as a process rather than a yes-or-no decision. Visibility and invisibility are not distinct opposites but are instead thought of as nuances between two poles, similar to the state of not being addressable or not being able to be found (Yamamoto-Masson 2014).

Another strategy of disappearing is to be seen too much. Obfuscation is an activist practice of producing too much noise and spreading misleading information, which can become a tool against surveillance (Brunton and Nissenbaum 2015). Disappearing becomes a political act not only in the decision to elude the regime of visibility but also in the sense of seeing it as a process of liberation. Beyond its function as a political tactic, becoming imperceptible or impersonal is the final form of becoming per se (Papadopoulos and Tsianos 2007). Disappearance is then a positive state of being from which one can act. As active practices, forms of disappearance and places of hiding can be read as tactics of disconnecting from the network and opting not to be seen anymore.

Disconnection Apps

Is your screen shimmering with different signals in all colors and shapes? Can you see one wireless carrier signal two meters away and another 230 meters away? Do you hear a noise that sounds like a Geiger counter in a nuclear power plant? Who wouldn't want to press the "get me out" button that stops it all and leads one to the nearest "dead zone." That is what you experience as a user of the White Spots App. Founded by information designer Richard Vijgen, the multimedia project not only visualizes the otherwise invisible electromagnetic waves of nearby surroundings but also indicates places without connection and therefore without radiation.

As White Spots illustrates, undoing networks is often mediated via digital technology in the form of yet another app. The large variety of disconnection applications can be divided into two main types, which are not necessarily mutually exclusive. There are those that form part of self-care practices and those for achieving a healthy work–life balance. Instead of a complete renouncement of digital media, these apps promote responsible, mindful usage. They help users block calls, messages, and sometimes even internet access; some can pause other apps for a self-chosen period (e.g. Offtime; Freedom); others even suggest mindfulness skills aimed at slowing down and becoming more focused (e.g. PAUSE).

Self-care practices often go hand-in-hand with the monitoring of users. As Melissa Gregg shows in her book *Counterproductive* (2018), there are also those apps that analyze user behavior while monitoring their screen time and tracking their clicks (e.g. Offtime; Apple's Screen time; Moment; QualityTime; Checky). In the realm of privacy and data protection, some apps offer antitracking instruments and VPN clients to guarantee anonymity while searching the web (e.g. Disconnect.me; AdGuard; NoTrack). Disconnection here becomes a technological process of self-care, as Google's recent Paper Phone experiment shows: Quite literally just a piece of paper, the Paper Phone lets you choose which information from your nonpaper phone you need for the day and then print it on real paper, which can be cut and folded to hold credit cards. This minimalistic version of your phone should help you be more "focused."

Doing Nothing

In his installation "Robot, doing nothing" for the 2017 Ars Electronica Festival in Linz, Austria, artist Emanuel Gollob created a robot that, as its name indicates, does nothing but move its arm back and forth. Standing in front of the robot, the observer's attention is captured by its repetitive movement and at the same time lulled by its aesthetic design. According to Gollob, the project "accuses our modern society of being incessantly busy even beyond the confines of everyday life in the workplace. What's now demanded of us—above all due to the proliferation of digital technologies—is our permanent presence, readiness to communicate and receptivity to information" (Gollob 2020).

Refusing to function as a particular part of society is hardly a new phenomenon. In predigital times, the decision to stop working—to strike—was already a political act, a refusal expressed against the ruling order of capital (Tronti 1966). As a timeless structure, a rupture in a chronology, the moment of doing nothing becomes a way of "falling out of the rhythm," as Stäheli (2014) describes it. There is also an infrastructural dimension to these non-events, which Ehn and Löfgren (2010) call "unglamorous events." "Doing nothing" can be seen as opting out of the norms of society and thereby, with the help of technologies, escaping it for a short period of time. One's lack of (social) value could become an act of critique in itself, inflecting the act of unplugging and doing nothing with a sense of active autonomy instead of seeing it as merely the other side of the call for connection. Moments of not functioning can be filled with pleasure, as in watching the robot's movements. Put this way, "doing nothing" becomes an aesthetic form of critique.

Electromagnetic Hypersensitivity (EHS)

What do you do when you are allergic to something that is found almost everywhere? Those who suffer from "electromagnetic hypersensitivity" (EHS) claim that they are sensitive to electromagnetic fields and waves at levels beyond the maximum permitted radiation. These sensitivities are said to arise particularly from Wi-Fi, radio, and mobile phones. Symptoms are said to include a general disposition to headaches, insomnia, and cell damage. To date, there have not been any successful scientific validations of patient claims to suffer from EHS, and it is not a recognized medical diagnosis by any countries or international organizations. One slight exception is Sweden, where EHS is recognized as a functional impairment but not a medical condition.

Those who self-identify as having EHS are often highly experienced in shielding themselves from electromagnetic waves. As well as protecting their body with shielding materials like metal foil and special textiles, their living spaces can become equipped with special baldachins draped over the bed, sleeping bags with silver threads or curtains for the windows. Carbon colors are used to paint the walls and keep out all traces of radiation. The market for these kinds of products is large, encompassing various devices that promise to "harmonize" electromagnetic fields by influencing the "vibrations" of electrons and protons. Special plugs promise to create an environment without radiation: once connected with the power circuit, they still allow the use of cell phones and Wi-Fi.

Finding a suitable place to live is especially difficult for people with EHS. Shielding a particular space is often not enough, and so they need to find a place where radiation is not as strong or does not exist at all. Personal reports on blogs illustrate how people with EHS organize their lives in dead zones. In most cases, this means sleeping in a caravan somewhere in the forest without electricity and water, always on the run from the nearest radio mast. Some claims of EHS exhibit a dangerous proximity to conspiracy theories: "deadly radiation" is one buzzword that is used by the same sects who also deny climate change and claim that Jews control the world.

Faraday Cage

What to do in case of a thunderstorm? Find a car or a plane and you will be safe. Because these are enclosures composed of a conductive material, their interiors are shielded from electric discharge. The exterior of the cage does not even have to be fully closed. As is the case with microwave ovens, a mesh is sufficient to keep radiation in (or out) because the holes in the net need only to be smaller than the length of the waves. Because of the wide range of frequencies, not every cage is radiation-proof, depending on the material of which it is made.

Faraday Cages were originally invented for the military and other organizations as a means of protecting vital IT or delicate electrical equipment from electromagnetic pulse attacks or lightning strikes. They are also used to shield from eavesdropping rooms where sensitive topics are being discussed. Because they block signals only passively, Faraday Cages are legal and there is a range of devices available for purchase on the open market. One look at Amazon reveals the most popular ways in which Faraday Cages are used: for shielding car keys, phones, and credit cards; or the "blackout-privacy protection security 6 pieces ultra-thick prepping kit" for more extensive protection.

Forest

In smartphone communication, data signals are digitized and transformed into high-frequency electromagnetic radiation. To transmit the signal, masts send electromagnetic waves to the respective receiver. The transmission depends on various factors including weather conditions and/or the conductivity of the earth or water; barriers and interferences can also prevent the radio wave from spreading. Along with factors like shadowing or reflection, absorption plays a major role in shaping transmission. Radio waves hit objects that absorb them. These objects can be buildings and plants, as well as the human body. The forest is one particularly large absorber, since it intercepts and dissipates radio waves through its leaves and branches.

As a result, forests can become hideouts for those who do not want to be found or want to escape electromagnetic radiation. Along with living in a digital society goes the idea of a transparent media and social space, in which everything and everybody can always be located. Disconnection—the act of opting out of digital networks—requires the creation of opaque locations, such as hideouts and other clandestine places (Stäheli 2014). The unplugged space is clandestine insofar as it evades digital control and visualization—it is not to be seen.

Since forests are often dead zones, it is no coincidence that they are also the site of a famous imaginary of disconnection in literature. In her novel *Notre vie dans les forêts* (2017)[4] Marie Darrieussecq paints a dystopian vision of a society where techno-capitalism has led to the robotization of all spheres of life, accompanied by total surveillance. A small group of rebels escapes to the forest from where they plan attacks on clone factories. As an offline world, the woods have become a symbol for primordial nature, somewhere mankind should return to. They are portrayed as the last place not touched by hyperconnectivity and therefore a good place to hide from drones and other surveillance technology.

Information Overload

The discourse of "information overload" occurs prominently in crisis diagnoses that call for disconnection. The term was coined in Alvin Toffler's popular scientific book *Future Shock* (1970). In 1965 Toffler had already stated that individuals are subject "to too much change in too short a time" (1970, 1; cited after Toffler 1965). Referring to major transformations in all realms of life (e.g., industrialization, new technologies, dissolution of classic family structures), Toffler pleads for taking the "disease of change" (1970, 1) seriously and offers "strategies for survival" (Toffler 1970, 369) for those who feel overwhelmed.

Today, the discourse of information overload does not refer to general societal change but rather to literally having too much information.[5] One argument made in popular discourse in favor of disconnecting holds that individuals are overwhelmed by the constant flow of information to which they are exposed in a world of ubiquitous online news, social media, and commercial screens. In "pre-digital times," people would apparently watch the news on public-service television once a day; they could trust that this newscast contained everything important that they needed to know and that public-service broadcasting was a reliable source. The same held true for the radio and for "serious" daily or weekly newspapers. In recent years, however, the number of news sources has multiplied. Aside from the sheer volume of news to which people are now exposed, one no longer knows which news sources can be trusted.

Proponents of the information overload discourse assert that "echo chambers" and "filter bubbles" have emerged on Facebook, where users receive targeted information which only confirms their already existent attitudes. They stress that the Cambridge Analytica scandal, which uncovered that Donald Trump and his team manipulated the 2016 electoral campaign by harvesting millions of Facebook profiles, led to great uncertainty concerning the reliability of news in general.

Like grocery stores, streaming services like Netflix and Spotify now demand that their users choose from an immense range of products, and what psychologists call the "freedom" or "burden of choice" is commonly seen as an overwhelming task. There is an interesting ambiguity in this particular information overload discourse. On the one hand, digital media seems like liberation: consumers are no longer tied to preselected broadcast programs and can actively decide what they want to watch, listen to, or read. On the other hand, the immense amount of options leads to exhaustion. Some people thus feel so overloaded with information that they decide to stop checking the news altogether. For them, this renunciation feels like the only way to regain their agency.

Internet Addiction

Like the discourse of information overload, the discourse of "internet addiction" is often used to argue for disconnection. In psychology, internet addiction emerged as a new nonchemical behavioral addiction (Marks 1990) in the 1990s, asserting that even though the internet is not a chemical drug, people show similar reactions to it. Psychologist Kimberly Young (1998) conducted a survey of internet addiction and then published a book on the phenomenon. It provides accounts of people who neglect their spouses and even forget to pick up their children because they are so consumed by chat rooms. In widespread reports about cases of online shopping addiction, online sex addiction, and online games addiction, one commonly reoccurring observation is that time spent online goes by faster than time spent offline.

Today, there are discussions of a new sub-syndrome of internet addiction: smartphone addiction. The slick way in which people unlock their phones in every spare second is reminiscent of the behavior of chain smokers who have perfected the art of efficiently lighting their cigarettes. Furthermore, there have been diagnoses of conditions like "WhatsAppitis," a specific form of "Repetitive-Strain-Injury-Syndrome" with symptoms including pain in one's thumbs and wrists caused by phone overuse. Another recent diagnosis is the "wired and tired" syndrome, also known as "adrenal fatigue." As the word "wired" suggests, it describes a state of general exhaustion caused by the stress of making connections and spending too much time on screens. Nevertheless, "internet addiction" is not recognized by the *Diagnostic and Statistical Manual of Mental Disorders* (DSM) (Sutton 2017).[6] Rather than a medically recognized condition, it can be understood as an element of popular discourse or a rhetorical tool used in pleas for disconnection.

The fear of media addiction has long been a common topos of media critique. In eighteenth-century Germany, there was a particularly heated debate about "Lesesucht" (reading mania) (Huyssen 1986; Littau 2006). People feared that spending too much time reading novels led to severe consequences: women were accused of neglecting their households, children, and husbands; men of developing revolutionary ideas. On top of these social risks, some even claimed that reading too many novels could cause physical diseases—just as too much food upsets the stomach, so can too many novels upset the brain.

Jamming

Jamming a signal means not merely blocking it but overriding the original signal by sending out broadband noise. In general, the higher the electrical capacity, the greater and wider the range of jamming frequencies. Jammers interfere with different frequencies, which range from radio waves, GPS signals, drones, and cellular signals to Bluetooth and Wi-Fi (possible even with low power). Some jamming is obvious, especially if it is audible; other jamming is subtler and silent. In another form of jamming known as "spoofing," incorrect GPS signals are sent to mislead the receiver.

Originating in the military, the practice of jamming was (and partly still is) used to prevent the reception of foreign signals, such as BBC broadcasts in Nazi Germany or Western broadcasts in the Soviet Union during the Cold War. Today, jamming used as an electronic counterstrategy remains a form of censorship, but it is also used to prevent the activation of bombs or for drone defense.

As an active disturbance of signals, jamming is illegal in most countries for members of the general population and is permitted only in official institutions such as prisons, among many other examples. Legal jammers can be found in public spaces like cinemas, theaters, or courts to inhibit disturbance caused by cell phone use. Regardless of their legal status, the open market offers a variety of jamming devices for everyday use, providing users with tools to prevent their car keys from being hacked, keep their credit cards safe, or even prevent a speed camera from triggering.

Besides radio jamming, "culture jamming" is used to describe an artistic performance that aims to subvert dominant representational norms. One widespread practice, known as *detournement,* is to alter advertisements to present a general critique of consumerism. Feminist artists like The Guerilla Girls also used it to criticize sexism in pop culture and the art world in general (Kuni 2012).

No Phones Allowed

Even if you manage to get into Berghain, Berlin's famously exclusive techno club, your phone's camera lenses will be covered with stickers. The photo ban, which can increasingly be found in other techno clubs, symbolizes the respect of personal boundaries as part of the emerging culture of "no phones allowed." It also ensures privacy, especially in a controversial space like Berghain, which builds on the tradition of sex-positivity in techno culture but also struggles to deal with its rapid popularity. With their roots in subcultural movements (D'Andrea 2007; St. John 2009), some techno and rave clubs, though having long arrived in the mainstream, still try to raise awareness about personal boundaries. Combined with the idea of enhancement in techno dance, enforcing a photo ban is not always an easy task. Although it mainly relies on the self-control and understanding of the guests, the club itself needs to organize the covering of the cameras and the communication of this rule.

While clubs enforcing a photo ban can reinforce their mythical image by not showing pictures of their interior, their guests can easily engage in subversive acts, such as secretly taking pictures in the toilets and putting them on Instagram. At the same time, the club's lens-covering stickers have become a symbol of belonging to a particular scene. After the party, people leave the stickers on their phones so that everybody can see where they spent the weekend. In this way, they become part of an imaginary collective of ravers who refuse to take pictures.

Clubs are not the only spaces where phones are not allowed. Other examples of phone bans are to be found in schools, courtrooms, during airplane take-offs and landings, and in some countries even in theaters and cinemas, to mention only some examples.

Spaces of disconnectivity are deeply embedded in power structures and hierarchies, as this example of their exclusivity shows. Nonetheless, they still contain the potential to create spaces of possibility, in which different desires can be acted out. In his preface to *The Order of Things,* Michel Foucault sketches out a new form of space as an unstable field within an otherwise finite distribution. In contrast to "utopias," "heterotopias" are located in different places, from where "they secretly undermine language" by forbidding common descriptions (Foucault 1994, xviii). For Foucault, the creation of a coherent space, as a search for a common tableau, is the establishment of an "order of things." A heterotopia exists as an area that deviates from order while at the same time indicating that there can be other orders; as an order in itself that at the same time represents the critique of the other. If unplugged spaces are seen as heterotopias, then they cannot simply be merged into connectivity, but are produced as liminal spaces of critique.

Offline

For analog nostalgists, being offline has great value. In a world where everything seems to be online, many feel that they can only lead an "authentic" life offline. The curation of everyday lives on social media, exemplified by the editing of pictures using filters on Instragam, leads to a certain distrust: If people's internet presence is assumed to be fake, then analog nostalgists feel that only when they meet people offline or "in real life" (irl) can they get to know their true, authentic selves. Face-to-face communication is taken to be more authentic than chatting via text messages, because offline conversations can be accompanied by blushing, stuttering, and other social cues that exceed the expressive capacity of emoji. These reactions, along with the mimicry of one's counterpart, is said to allow for authentic communication.

The word "offline" is especially popular in Germany in the context of imaginaries of digital disconnection. The teenage novel *The Other Side of Lost* by Jessi Kirby (2018) has been translated into German as *Offline ist es nass, wenn's regnet* (2019), meaning "offline it is wet when it's raining." But "offline" does not have exclusively positive connotations: the German psycho-thriller *Offline* (2019) by Arno Strobel follows a group of people who go on a digital detox trip to the mountains, which becomes a horror trip when one of the participants disappears and is then found severely abused. Being offline represents the downfall of the novel's protagonists.

On Instagram, there are currently around 481,000 posts tagged #offline.[7] The images gathered under this hashtag include pictures not only of nature, families, pets, and people announcing that they are going offline for a certain period of time, but also of people eating. There are even selfies of people in #offline elevators. Thus, the hashtag seems to be used for any kind of activity that doesn't take place directly in front of a computer—it takes on the form of an empty signifier whose total emptiness simultaneously means total abundance (Laclau 2007).

Perturbation

When riding public transportation, one sometimes doubts the diagnosis of "ubiquitous connectivity." Even on Germany's celebrated national railroad system, phone calls are interrupted as soon as the train enters a tunnel (and sometimes without any recognizable reason at all). On Germany's high-speed train, the Intercity-Express's (ICE), the on-board Wi-Fi service is so unreliable that sending an e-mail becomes a real challenge. These experiences cannot be described as moments of disconnectivity; they are moments of perturbation.

Whereas "perturbation" describes some kind of unintended mistake—a failure, malfunction, or shortcoming—"disconnection" always involves intentional practices, which are not deficient but distinct. In contrast to perturbation, disconnectivity needs to be actively produced. Passing a dead zone in a train and becoming annoyed at a poor signal is different than deliberately visiting dead zones for a digital detox vacation. Whereas the former example describes a case of perturbation, the latter describes a case of disconnection. Still, this distinction between perturbation and disconnection should not reproduce the dualism between technological determinism on the one hand and the idea of the autonomous human on the other.

Moments of perturbation do not necessarily mean being completely at the mercy of (malfunctioning) technology. Neither do moments of disconnection require the human subject to regain agency. Following this logic would amount to agreeing with proponents of Digital Detox and Digital Minimalism who believe that human beings are fundamentally threatened by technology. Rather, disconnection can be understood as a heterogenous material process that involves humans and technological infrastructures as well as imaginaries.

Renunciation

It has become almost impossible to renounce digital media completely. It is hard to imagine someone pursuing a career without an e-mail address. University students who do not own laptops will not be able to write and hand in much of their coursework.[8] And ironically, even digital detox trips have to be booked online. Yet there are still people who are not on social media and who do not use smartphones. Some of them do not have to "renounce" digital media because they have never used it in the first place; others were once keen internet enthusiasts who changed their minds. In one of many examples of repentance among former social media enthusiasts, Chamath Palihapitiya, a senior executive at Facebook from 2007 to 2011, said that he now feels "tremendous guilt" about having helped to build up the company. He states that Facebook is "ripping apart the social fabric of how society works" by its "short-term, dopamine-driven feedback loops." In a talk at the Stanford Graduate School of Business, Palihapitiya recommends that people take a "hard break" from social media (Vincent 2017). Karppi and Nieborg (2020) identify these confessions as "corporate abdication." The confessions of former Facebook employees "are not so much truths about these technologies and how the platform actually functions, but rather efforts to construct and shape our vision of platform power by mapping and highlighting particular relations instead of others" (Karppi and Nieborg 2020, 5).

There is a story about Bay Area employees who work in Silicon Valley but send their children to Waldorf schools because they are free of mobile phones (Nathani 2018). The fact that the very people who warn against hyperconnectivity and recommend disconnection are internet and technology experts might make their advice appear particularly credible. They may appear to know more about the addictive nature of the technology that they, after all, developed themselves. One of the most prominent and influential critics of social media is computer scientist Jaron Lanier, one of the developers of virtual reality. Cal Newport, author of *Digital Minimalism,* is also a professor of computer science. The statements of experts like these can be understood as one specific discourse of disconnection among others, including those of media scholars, psychologists, and analog nostalgists. By using rhetorical devices related to "internet addiction" and "saving the children," these experts construct one specific perspective on social media.

Right to Disconnect

The "right to disconnect" is intended to protect employees from constant availability by assuring them that they do not have to check their e-mails or answer phone calls during nonworking hours. "Le droit à la déconnexion," as this right is called in the country where it originated, is a response to the dissolving of boundaries between work time and free time. The right to disconnect emerged in France in 2001 as a means of assuring employees they are not obliged to work at home or to take home their files and office equipment. With the advent of smartphones, the need for this right became even more pressing. In 2016, the "El Khomri Law" (named after France's then-current Minister of Labor) was passed by the national government, offering French employees the right to disconnect from work calls and e-mails during nonworking hours (Collins et al. 2019). A paragraph was added to the law that specified how to proceed if an employer fails to respect the employee's right to personal and family time (e.g., implementing training and awareness-raising activities regarding the reasonable use of digital tools) (Legifrance 2016). The right took legal effect on January 1, 2017.

In recent years, other countries, including the Philippines, Italy, Spain, and Canada, have implemented similar rights. In addition to legal enforcement, some companies have introduced policies that stop e-mail servers from sending e-mails to mobile phones after a certain time of day. Pepita Hesselberth (2018) focuses on the debate around the right to disconnect in order to study the paradox of dis/connectivity. She points out that the above-mentioned amendments made to the "El Khomri Law" risk having the opposite effect of what they aim to achieve. In declaring that the "penalty" imposed on the employer when violating the employee's right to disconnect consists in implementing awareness training, the law becomes neither mandatory nor binding. Thus, the traditional separation between work time and free time is not necessarily retained; the risk is that every hour of the employee's life becomes available for the employer to access. Rather than concluding that there is "no outside" to the "culture of connectivity" (van Dijck 2013), Hesselbert argues, similarly to Tero Karppi (2018), that disconnectivity simultaneously limits and constitutes connectivity; therein lies the paradox of dis/connectivity.

Shield Wear

Shield wear refers to clothes and jewelry made of material that blocks radio waves and wireless signals, or makes one invisible to surveillance drones and face-recognition cameras. It might also protect those who believe in the harmfulness of electromagnetic radiation. Artists like Nicole Scheller (interviewed in this book), Adam Harvey, and Ewa Nowak make it their project to create this kind of privacy fashion. They experiment with materials and forms so as not only to make political statements but to make them fashionable. Some of these clothes are built after the Faraday cage principle, so that the person wearing the garment is shielded from an electromagnetic field. Others have a built-in reflection shield that blinds cameras (also by using light) and is capable of thermal reflection, so that the wearer is not visible on infrared cameras. In addition to such blocking materials, another way of avoiding one's biological data being analyzed is to change the body's shape and camouflage the face through distorted shapes and patterns and unnatural proportions of masks, paint, or jewelry.

 Shield wear is not necessarily emancipatory, but companies also sell shield wear for formal use. The Dutch company Holland Shielding Systems BV offers a collection of materials that protect the body from electromagnetic fields. One item is the shielded burka, advertised on the company's website as follows: "Shielding your head just got easier. Slip this sheer and roomy burka over your head and it will provide 99.7% shielding across the frequency range 10 MHz—3 GHz and > 94% at 5.6 GHz. These frequencies include Wi-Fi, cordless phones, phone masts, mobile phones, and even TV and radio broadcasts. . . . Quick to put on, easy to take off. One size fits all" (Holland Shielding Systems BV 2020). Considering the debate around banning face veils in various European countries and the oppressive character ascribed to burkas for some Islamic women who wear them, this lighthearted advertisement appears quite odd. One wonders if the company accidentally adopted an inappropriate tone or if it can be understood as a deliberate revaluation of the burka: instead of being compulsory, the shielded burka is now easy to put on and remove. It is not designed for women alone but according to the principles of one-size-fits-all. Its purpose is not to protect women from the male gaze or to protect men from the sight of female bodies but to protect everyone from electromagnetic fields. The depicted item (https://hollandshielding.com/Shielded-burka?_ga=2.225674202.1981716146.1605613357-2099775437.1605613357) is actually a niqaab rather than a burka—the latter covers not only the head but the whole body, with only a mesh screen in front of the eyes. Thus, shield wear forms part of a wider debate around concealment practices; this debate covers issues related to emancipatory practices as well as commercialization.

Social Distancing

It is still too early to estimate the long-term effects of the current Covid-19 pandemic on disconnection discourses and the field of disconnection studies (and there are, of course, much more pressing issues at the moment). However, it is already clear that a fundamental shift is taking place (as of March 23, 2020). The form of "connectedness"[9] celebrated by analog nostalgists and proponents of digital detox cannot currently be enjoyed, since people are asked (or in some countries obliged) to stay at home. The Digital Detox® website announces that the "May 2020 Camp is Cancelled Due to COVID-19 Travel Concerns" (Digital Detox 2020). On Instagram the hashtags #stayhome, #stayathome, or, more aggressively, #staythefuckhome enjoy great popularity. To slow down the dissemination of the virus, we need to practice "social distancing."

The plea for social distancing is very different from the plea for digital detox. Whereas discourses arguing for digital detox are likely to favor human encounters but fear that digital technologies pose a threat to "real" connections, in times of social distancing communication technologies are the only way to stay in touch with friends, family members, and colleagues. Will the internet's reputation, even among analog nostalgists, benefit from the coronavirus crisis?

To avoid connotations of isolation, the World Health Organization has started to use the term "physical distancing," which was proposed by Daniel Aldrich, a U.S. professor of political science and public policy (Gale 2020). In Germany, there is also the notion of "Kontaktverbot" (usually meaning a "restraining order," albeit the literal translation is "prohibition of contact"). When googling the term, one can read headlines concerning numerous breaches of the "Kontaktverbot" that were punished by the police. Thus, new (moralizing) discourses around how to behave have emerged in light of the crisis; their semantics differ greatly across contexts and countries.

Aside from this possible revaluation of the internet in the context of cultural-critical discourses on digital technologies, along with the emergence of new discourses of disconnection, the current situation sheds light on the societal importance of distance. As early as 1903, Georg Simmel (1950) pointed to the fact that social distancing is a key coping mechanism for people living in big cities.[10] Only by keeping fellow urbanites and the constant flow of impressions at bay can life in a big city become possible without being constantly overwhelmed. Whereas recent decades were marked by a “fetish of connectivity” (Pedersen 2013, quoted by Stäheli at the start of chapter 1 of this volume), the current crisis highlights the risks and limits of connectivity. It is to be expected that our current state of social distancing will affect the way we conceive of society as such. Approaches that manage to conceptualize moments of disconnectivity and distance will therefore only be in greater demand.

Unfollowing

Ubiquitous connectivity affects not only the way we date (e.g., using apps like Grindr or Tinder) but also the way we break up (Gershon 2012). Urs Stäheli (2013) refers to an interesting German blog entry written in 2012 under the heading “Die emotionale Entnetzung—Trennung in Zeiten des Internets” (Undoing networks in emotional terms: Separation in the internet age). In the post, blogger FrolleinSocial (2012) describes the cumbersome process of separating from her ex-boyfriend. Formerly, the only “account” that needed to be deleted was the ex-partner’s name on the shared doorbell nameplate. Information relating to the ex-partner’s life could be provided by mutual friends (ideally, upon request only). Nowadays, the process of separation is much more laborious. Precautions must actively be taken if one is not to be permanently inundated with details about the ex-partner’s life. There are several platforms (e.g., Facebook, Instagram, Twitter) on which FrolleinSocial needs to actively block her ex-boyfriend’s account. A more radical approach is to “unfriend” (Facebook) or “unfollow” (Instagram and Twitter) him. According to Stäheli (2013, 4), this blog entry illustrates how the cutting of ties is a cumbersome process that becomes even more tedious in the internet age, as connections proliferate to an unprecedented degree.

“Unfollow” is also the name of an app and the title of a recently published German bestselling book (Schink 2020). The app serves to track people who have unfollowed you on Instagram (following someone in order to make them follow you back, only to have them then unfollow you in order to get more followers of their own—this seems to be a socially undesirable yet recurrent phenomenon on Instagram). The book, on the other hand, is a furious critique of Instagram (its subtitle is *Wie Instagram unser Leben zerstört,* or "How Instagram is destroying our lives"). Even though the app and the book share the same title, they have opposite agendas, both of which are characteristic of current discourses on (dis)connectivity. Whereas the app represents the desire to enhance one's popularity in terms of the number of Instagram followers and mobilizes the fear of losing these followers, the book questions the overall logic of following and advocates unfollowing.

Unfriending

"Unfriending" (John and Dvir-Gvirsman 2015; Schwarz and Shani 2016; Sibona and Walzak 2011; John and Gal 2018) is an activity exclusively associated with Facebook, insofar as the people users are connected with are not called "friends" but "followers" on other social media platforms like Instagram and Twitter. Nicholas A. John and Noam Gal argue that Facebook is "by far the most popular social media platform in Israel" (2018, 2971). Based on interviews with Jewish Israeli Facebook users, John and Gal explore the political connotations of unfriending someone on Facebook during the Israel–Gaza conflict of 2014. According to John and Gal, unfriending is a "form of [online] boundary management for the self in conditions of networked sociality" (2971). The authors develop the "productive . . . oxymoron" of the "personal public sphere" (2971) as a means of theorizing the communicative space for political discussion emerging on social networking sites. In their research, John and Gal notice a certain dissonance: to achieve the desired effect (i.e., removing certain political posts from their newsfeeds), their interviewees could simply have hidden unwanted posts of their Facebook friends instead of unfriending them altogether. Acknowledging this dissonance, John and Gal conclude that unfriending can be understood as "the exercise of sovereignty over the personal public sphere" (2982), and argue further that "the issue of with whom I am connected" (2973) is an important aspect of identity-building.

Comparing their findings to the act of "unfollowing" points to a qualitative difference between the two modes of undoing online ties. Do social relations on Facebook tend to follow a pattern of constant reciprocity and mutual identification while ties on Instagram take a more ephemeral shape?

Unplugging

"Unplugging," as a practice of disconnection, means actively withdrawing—usually only temporarily—from the state of being digitally connected. The decision to "opt out" is often accompanied by events that celebrate the peculiarity of the act itself: smiling, happy people hold signs saying "I unplug to . . . reconnect, jam, love, cherish the moment, go party, sleep all day" and so on.

Starting in 2010, the National Day of Unplugging in the United States has called the first Friday in every March for "a 24-hour respite from technology" (National Day of Unplugging). Associated with the Jewish sabbath tradition, this initiative from a nonprofit Jewish organization known as "Reboot" wrote a corresponding "Sabbath Manifesto" for the digital world. Combining religious rules with the slow movement, it is based on ten main principles: "avoid technology; connect with loved ones; nurture your health; get outside; avoid commerce; light candles; drink wine; eat bread; find silence; give back" (Sabbath Manifesto). Rooted in the religious rules of the Sabbath (which does not allow Jewish people to use electrical devices), the discussion around temporary digital abstinence becomes detached from its religious origins and develops into a conception of self-care in general.

In addition to foregoing use of technological devices, participants in National Day of Unplugging can further engage by hosting events such as unplugged bike rides or phone-free community dinners. There is even a program for unplugging with children (because "they are born unplugged"), providing the "unplugger" with boxes that contain a "cell phone sleeping bag," ideas for board games, and cooking recipes.

When used in the field of education, unplugging becomes a long-term strategy, evident in the concept of "unplugged classrooms," whereby phones are banned from schools. Aside from institutional unplugging, as in schools and courtrooms, most unplugged spaces are hidden or not easy to find. With a little effort, however, a broad range of these spaces can be revealed, including phone-free clubs, coffee shops, and fancy restaurants where one is not allowed to use one's phone. The process of becoming unplugged requires a highly complex organizational structure and the help of technologies, practices, and infrastructures.

Notes

We would like to thank Timon Beyes, Tero Karppi, and Urs Stäheli for their help with developing this glossary. Further, we thank Erik Born and Sean Shields for their copyediting work and their helpful comments as well as Finn Brunton and Melissa Gregg for their substantial reviews.

1 See Sterne 2016 for a critique of this simplified notion of analog media.
2 See Sutton 2017 as well as Stäheli and Stoltenberg 2020 for research on this particular camp.
3 As of today (March 30, 2020) the website has disappeared. Seppukoo can only be accessed via http://www.seppukoo.com/how-it-works.
4 English title: *Our Life in the Forest.*
5 See Mark Andrejevic's book *Infoglut* (2013).
6 Nick Seaver (2019) suggests using anthropological theories about trapping when thinking about algorithmic recommender systems. He argues that the notion of the trap offers an alternative to the moralizing framings of internet addiction.
7 See Jorge 2019, whose discourse analysis of temporary disconnection on Instagram includes the hashtag #offline.
8 The questions of unequal access to digital technologies are discussed in debates on the "digital divide"; see, among others, Norris 2001.
9 José van Dijck (2013) distinguishes between "connectedness" and "connectivity." Whereas the latter describes connections commodified by social-networking

companies, the former refers to the "genuine" human desire to connect with one another.

10 See Urs Stäheli's contribution in this volume as well as Stäheli 2018.

References

Andrejevic, Mark. 2013. *Infoglut. How Too Much Information Is Changing the Way We Think and Know.* New York: Routledge.

Brewis, Joanna, and Christopher Grey. 2008. "The Regulation of Smoking at Work." *Human Relations* 61, no. 7: 965–87.

Brunton, Finn, and Helen Nissenbaum. 2015. *Obfuscation: A User's Guide for Privacy and Protest.* London: MIT Press.

Collins, Erica C., Daniel Ornstein, and Jordan B. Glassberg. 2019. "More Countries Consider Implementing a 'Right to Disconnect.'" *The National Law Review,* January 29. Accessed April 21, 2020. https://www.natlawreview.com/article/more-countries-consider-implementing-right-to-disconnect.

D'Andrea, Anthony. 2007. *Global Nomads: Techno and New Age as Transnational Countercultures in Ibiza and Goa.* London: Routledge.

Darrieussecq, Marie. 2017. *Notre Vie dans les Forêts.* Paris: Editions P.O.L.

Digital Detox®. 2020. *Official Website.* Accessed April 21, 2020. www.digitaldetox.com.

Ehn, Billy, and Orvar Löfgren. 2010. *The Secret World of Doing Nothing.* Berkeley: University of California Press.

Fish, Adam. 2017. "Technology Retreats and the Politics of Social Media." *TripleC* 15, no. 1: 355–69.

Foucault, Michel. 1994. *The Order of Things.* New York: Random House.

FrolleinSocial. 2012. "Die emotionale Entnetzung—Trennung in Zeiten des Internets." *FrolleinSocial,* September 13. Accessed April 21, 2020. https://frolleinsocial.wordpress.com/2012/09/13/die-emotionale-entnetzung-trennung-in-zeiten-des-internets/.

Gale, Rebecca. 2020. "Is 'Social Distancing' the Wrong Term? Expert Prefers 'Physical Distancing', and the WHO Agrees." *The Washington Post,* March 26. Accessed April 21, 2020. https://www.washingtonpost.com/lifestyle/wellness/social-distancing-coronavirus-physical-distancing/2020/03/25/a4d4b8bc-6ecf-11ea-aa80-c2470c6b2034_story.html.

Gershon, Ilana. 2012. *The Breakup 2.0: Disconnecting over New Media.* Ithaca, N.Y.: Cornell University Press.

Gollob, Emanuel. 2020. *Official Website.* Accessed April 21, 2020. http://www.emanuelgollob.com.

Gregg, Melissa. 2018. *Counterproductive: Time Management in the Knowledge Economy.* Durham, N.C.: Duke University Press.

Hesselberth, Pepita. 2018. "Discourses on Disconnectivity and the Right to Disconnect." *New Media & Society* 20, no. 5: 1994–2010.

Holland Shielding Systems BV. 2020. "Buy Our Shielded Burka." Accessed April 21, 2020. https://hollandshielding.com/Shielded-burka.

Huyssen, Andreas. 1986. "Mass Culture as Woman: Modernism's Other." In *Studies in Entertainment: Critical Approaches to Mass Culture,* ed. Tania Modleski, 188–208. Bloomington: Indiana University Press.

John, Nicholas A., and Shira Dvir-Gvirsman. 2015. "'I Don't Like You Any More': Facebook Unfriending by Israelis During the Israel–Gaza Conflict of 2014." *Journal of Communication* 65, no. 6: 953–74.

John, Nicholas A., and Noam Gal. 2018. "'He's Got His Own Sea': Political Facebook Unfriending in the Personal Public Sphere." *International Journal of Communication* 12:2971–88.

Jorge, Ana. 2019. "Social Media, Interrupted: Users Recounting Temporary Disconnection on Instagram." *Social Media + Society* 5, no. 4. https://doi.org/10.1177/2056305119881691.

Jurgenson, Nathan. 2013. "The Disconnectionists." *The New Inquiry.* Accessed April 21, 2020. https://thenewinquiry.com/the-disconnectionists/.

Karppi, Tero. 2011. "Digital Suicide and the Biopolitics of Leaving Facebook." *Transformations Journal of Media & Culture* 20:1–18. http://www.transformationsjournal.org/wp-content/uploads/2016/12/Karppi_Trans20.pdf.

Karppi, Tero. 2018. *Disconnect. Facebook's Affective Bonds.* Minneapolis: University of Minnesota Press.

Karppi, Tero, and Nieborg, David B. 2020. "Facebook Confessions: Corporate Abdication and Silicon Valley Dystopianism." *New Media & Society,* June 2020: 1–16. https://doi.org/10.1177/1461444820933549

Kirby, Jessi. 2018. *The Other Side of Lost.* New York: Harper Collins. German translation: *Offline ist es nass, wenn's regnet: Digital Detox Roman.* Bindlach: Loewe Verlag, 2019.

Kuni, Verena. 2012. "Gender Jamming. Or: Yes, We Are. Culture Jamming and Feminism." In *Feminist Media: Participatory Spaces, Networks and Cultural Citizenship,* ed. Elke Zobel and Ricarda Drüeke, 98–109. Bielefeld: transcript Verlag.

Laclau, Ernesto. 2007 [1996]. "Why Do Empty Signifiers Matter to Politics?" In *Emancipation(s),* ed. Ernesto Laclau, 36–46. London: Verso.

Legifrance. 2016. "LOI n° 2016–1088 du 8 août 2016 relative au travail, à la modernisation du dialogue social et à la sécurisation des parcours professionnels (1). Chapitre II." *JORF n°0184 du 9 août 2016, Texte N° 3.* Accessed April 21, 2020. https://www.legifrance.gouv.fr/eli/loi/2016/8/8/ETSX1604461L/jo#JORFSCTA000032983228.

Littau, Karin. 2006. *Theories of Reading: Books, Bodies, and Bibliomania.* Cambridge, U.K.: Polity Press.

Markovinovic, Monika. 2019. "Digital Detox Beauty Products. Offline Time." *Montecristo Magazine,* June 3. Accessed April 21, 2020. https://montecristomagazine.com/magazine/spring-2019/digital-detox-beauty-products.

Marks, Isaac. 1990. "Behavioural (Non-chemical) Addictions." *British Journal of Addiction* 85, no. 11: 1389–94.

Marks, Laura U. 2012. *Touch: Sensuous Theory and Multisensory Media.* Minneapolis: University of Minnesota Press.

Massumi, Brian. 2015. *Politics of Affect.* Cambridge, U.K.: Polity Press.

Mejias, Ulises Ali. 2013. *Off the Network: Disrupting the Digital World.* Minneapolis: University of Minnesota Press.

Nathani, Komal. 2018. "The Techpreneurs of Silicon Valley Are Keeping Their Families Away from Technology. Should You Too?" *Entrepreneur,* August 30. Accessed April 21, 2020. https://www.entrepreneur.com/article/319288.

National Day of Unplugging. Accessed April 21, 2020. https://www.nationaldayofunplugging.com/.

Newport, Cal. 2006. *How to Become a Straight-A Student: The Unconventional Strategies Real College Students Use to Score High While Studying Less.* New York: Broadway Books.

Newport, Cal. 2016. *Deep Work: Rules for Focused Success in a Distracted World.* New York: Hachette Book Group.

Newport, Cal. 2019. *Digital Minimalism: On Living Better with Less Technology.* New York: Penguin Random House.

Newport, Cal. 2020. "Study Hacks Blog." *Cal Newport's Official Website.* Accessed April 21, 2020. https://www.calnewport.com/blog/.

Niche Beauty. n.d. "Amly Botanicals. City Screen Face Serum." *Online Shop.* Accessed April 21, 2020. https://www.niche-beauty.com/en-de/products/amly-botanicals-city-screen-face-serum/323-005.

Norris, Pippa. 2001. *Digital Divide: Civic Engagement, Information Poverty, and the Internet Worldwide.* Cambridge: Cambridge University Press.

Papadopoulos, Dimitris, and Vassilis Tsianos. 2007. "The Autonomy of Migration: The Animals of Undocumented Mobility." In *Deleuzian Encounters: Studies in Contemporary Social Issues,* ed. Anna Hickey-Moody and Peta Malins, 223–35. Basingstoke, U.K.: Palgrave Macmillan.

Pedersen, Morten A. 2013. "The Fetish of Connectivity." In *Objects and Materials: A Routledge Companion,* ed. Gilian Evans, Elizabeth B. Silva, and Nicholas Thoburn, 197–207. London: Routledge.

Peters, Benjamin. 2016. "Digital." In *Digital Keywords: A Vocabulary of Information Society and Culture,* 93–108. Princeton, N.J.: Princeton University Press.

Portwood-Stacer, Laura. 2013. "Media Refusal and Conspicuous Non-consumption: The Performative and Political Dimensions of Facebook Abstention." *New Media & Society* 15, no. 7: 1041–57.

Sabbath Manifesto. n.d. Accessed April 21, 2020. http://www.sabbathmanifesto.org/.

Schink, Nena. 2020. *Unfollow! Wie Instagram unser Leben zerstört.* München: C. H. Beck.

Schrey, Dominik. 2014. "Analogue Nostalgia and the Aesthetics of Digital Remediation." In *Media and Nostalgia: Yearning for the Past, Present, and Future,* ed. Katharina Niemeyer, 27–38. Basingstoke, U.K.: Palgrave Macmillan.

Schwarz, Ori, and Guy Shani. 2016. "Culture in Mediated Interaction: Political Defriending on Facebook and the Limits of Networked Individualism." *American Journal of Cultural Sociology* 4, no. 3: 385–421.

Seaver, Nick. 2019. "Captivating Algorithms: Recommender Systems as Traps." *Journal of Media Culture* 24, no. 4: 421–36.

Seppukoo. 2009. *Official Website.* Accessed March 1, 2020. http://www.seppukoo.com.

Sibona, Christopher, and Steven Walczak. 2011. "Unfriending on Facebook: Friend Request and Online/Offline Behavior Analysis." Paper presented at the 44th Hawaii International Conference on System Sciences Koloa, HI.

Simmel, Georg. 1950 [1903]. "The Metropolis and Mental Life." In *The Sociology of Georg Simmel,* trans. and ed. Kurt H. Wolff, 409–24. New York: Free Press.

Stäheli, Urs. 2013. "Entnetzt euch! Praktiken und Ästhetiken der Anschlusslosigkeit." *Mittelweg* 36:3–28.

Stäheli, Urs. 2014. "Aus dem Rhythmus fallen: Zur öffentlichen Entnetzung." *Kursbuch* 177:66–77.

Stäheli, Urs. 2018. "Distanz und Indifferenz." *Georg Simmel und das Leben in der Gegenwart,* ed. Rüdiger Lautmann and Hanns Wienold, 169–91. Wiesbaden: Springer VS.

Stäheli, Urs, and Luise Stoltenberg. 2020. "Digital Detox Tourism: Practices of Analogization." Submitted to *New Media & Society.*

Sterne, Jonathan. 2016. "Analog." In *Digital Keywords: A Vocabulary of Information Society and Culture,* ed. Benjamin Peters, 31–44. Princeton, N.J.: Princeton University Press.

Steyerl, Hito. 2013. "How Not to Be Seen. A Fucking Didactic Educational .MOV File." Accessed April 21, 2020. https://www.artforum.com/video/hito-steyerl-how-not-to-be-seen-a-fucking-didactic-educational-mov-file-2013-51651.

St. John, Graham. 2009. *Technomad: Global Raving Countercultures.* Sheffield, U.K.: Equinox Publishing.

Strobel, Arno. 2019. *Offline—Du wolltest nicht erreichbar sein: Jetzt sitzt du in der Falle.* Frankfurt am Main: Fischer Verlag.

Sundén, Jenny. 2018. "Queer Disonnections: Affect, Break, and Delay in Digital Connectivity." *Transformations* 31:63–78.

Sutton, Theodora. 2017. "Disconnect to Reconnect: The Food/Technology Metaphor in Digital Detoxing." *First Monday* 22, no. 6. Accessed April 21, 2020. https://doi.org/10.5210/fm.v22i6.7561.

Toffler, Alvin. 1965. "The Future as a Way of Life." *Horizon* 7, no. 3: 450–61.

Toffler, Alvin. 1970. *Future Shock.* New York: Random House.

Tronti, Mario. 1966. "The Strategy of the Refusal." In *Operai e Capitale* ("Workers and Capital")," 234–52. Turin: Einaudi.

Van Dijck, José. 2013. *The Culture of Connectivity: A Critical History of Social Media.* Oxford: Oxford University Press.

Yamamoto-Masson, Nine. 2014. "On Disappearance—σ and Strategic Withdrawal from Surface Monitoring." *Official Website.* Accessed April 21, 2020. https://nineyamamotomasson.com/disappearance.

Vincent, James. 2017. "Former Facebook Exec Says Social Media Is Ripping Apart Society." *The Verge,* December 11. Accessed April 21, 2020. https://www.theverge.com/2017/12/11/16761016/former-facebook-exec-ripping-apart-society.

Young, Kimberly S. 1998. "Internet Addiction: The Emergence of a New Clinical Disorder." *CyberPsychology and Behavior* 1, no. 3: 237–44.

Authors

Tero Karppi is assistant professor at the University of Toronto. He teaches in the Institute of Communication, Culture, Information, and Technology and in the Faculty of Information. He is author of *Disconnect: Facebook's Affective Bonds* (Minnesota, 2018).

Urs Stäheli is professor of sociology and sociological theory at the University of Hamburg, Germany. He is author of *Spectacular Speculation: Thrills, the Economy, and Popular Discourse,* among other books.

Clara Wieghorst is a research associate and PhD student at the Center for Digital Cultures and the Institute of Sociology and Cultural Organization at Leuphana University Lüneburg.

Lea P. Zierott is a research associate and PhD student in the Department of Social Sciences at the University of Hamburg.